Economics: Current and Future Developments

(Volume 2)

(Pluralist Readings in Economics: Key Concepts and Policy Tools for the 21st Century)

Authored by

Maria Alejandra Madi
World Economics Association, State University of Campinas, Av. Angelica 1711, cj. 111, São Paulo, Brazil

General:

1. Any dispute or claim arising out of or in connection with this License Agreement or the Work (including non-contractual disputes or claims) will be governed by and construed in accordance with the laws of the U.A.E. as applied in the Emirate of Dubai. Each party agrees that the courts of the Emirate of Dubai shall have exclusive jurisdiction to settle any dispute or claim arising out of or in connection with this License Agreement or the Work (including non-contractual disputes or claims).
2. Your rights under this License Agreement will automatically terminate without notice and without the need for a court order if at any point you breach any terms of this License Agreement. In no event will any delay or failure by Bentham Science Publishers in enforcing your compliance with this License Agreement constitute a waiver of any of its rights.
3. You acknowledge that you have read this License Agreement, and agree to be bound by its terms and conditions. To the extent that any other terms and conditions presented on any website of Bentham Science Publishers conflict with, or are inconsistent with, the terms and conditions set out in this License Agreement, you acknowledge that the terms and conditions set out in this License Agreement shall prevail.

Bentham Science Publishers Ltd.
Executive Suite Y - 2
PO Box 7917, Saif Zone
Sharjah, U.A.E.
Email: subscriptions@benthamscience.org

BENTHAM
SCIENCE

CONTENTS

FOREWORD

The complexity of social and economic policy problems of the 21st century, including the widening of inequality gaps both locally and globally, is strongly increasing. Many take this as a call to revise, in a nontrivial way, our conceptual outlooks, and to increase recognition of the role and importance of multi-sided reflection of theory and practice. The evolution of capitalism and the globalization of its various forms has contributed to unprecedented social, political, and environmental challenges. The global financial crisis of 2007-2008 made clear the need to redress and redesign both the global economy and economics as a discipline, to broadening the dialogue on social responsibility, and to develop a new culture of decision making. The long-standing debates regarding economic systems, criteria of economic and social justice, and which macroeconomic policies bring about the best possible outcomes are gaining currency; this leads to asking new questions concerning various aspects of the state and market relationships on national and transnational levels, and the relation between freedom and capital economy. A pluralist approach is needed, both practically and methodologically, for a better grasp of the historical development and conditions of both the current socio-economic system and our framing and perception of it in problem solving approaches.

Pluralist Readings in Economics: Key-concepts and policy tools for the 21st century provides such conceptual openings in interdisciplinary engaged and accessible ways. In this eBook, Maria Alejandra Madi provides broad coverage of the topics through a careful selection of some of the influential economic thinkers, and offers a substantial literature overview that includes pointing the reader to the main tenets of the included authors' ideas, context, and interpretations. Dealing with complex problems requires an ability to go beyond our received ideas and conceptualizations of the problems in question to redefine them in new contexts, and to dialoguing on social responsibility. Maria Alejandra Madi's introductory work fits well with such end, preparing the reader for enlargement of the debate that aims to contribute to the transformation to a more just and sustainable economy and world.

The book is recommended for a broad interdisciplinary audience, specifically to students in social sciences and humanities. It will benefit all those who seek to better understand the complex stakes in the transitions of the capitalist system, in the tensions between regulatory policies, free market equilibria, and participatory openings in governance.

Malgorzata Dereniowska
Aix-Marseille University, Marseille,
France

PREFACE

As John Kenneth Galbraith pointed out economics is overwhelmed by an *'uncorrected obsolescence.'* The target of economics education is the comprehension of the reality in its economic dimension, that is to say, the understanding of those practices and ideas that support the evolution of material life and the provision of human needs. In the post-war period, economics was broadly understood as economic science, that is to say, as a specific area of the development of human knowledge. Today, the main challenge to economics as a discipline is to cope with changing economic realities. In the current setting, a pluralist approach to economics attempts to consider a broad scope of perspectives in order to apprehend the complexity of the real-world.

These *Pluralist Readings* aim to foster the awareness of diversity of ideas within economic thought. Its scope involves broad topics in economics and debates about historical and theoretical approaches, besides policy matters. We examine the contribution of major thinkers in relation to their understanding of the historical development of capitalism, highlighting the writings of Karl Polanyi. Rudolf Hilferding and Eric Hobsbawm. Indeed, at the heart of modern political thought there is an ongoing debate about the main features and the outcomes of the capitalist system. Considering the power issues at stake in the capital accumulation process, relevant questions have emerged in the economic debate. At this respect, we include the writings of scientists who sharply analysed the conflicts and tensions within the economic capitalist system, including Karl Marx, Michal Kalecki and John Kenneth Galbraith.

Significant contributions to monetary theory by Eugen von Böhm-Bawerk, John Maynard Keynes and James Tobin are also considered. Indeed, controversies about the role of money, interest rates and the banking system have been present in economic debates since the 18th century. Today, monetary issues continue to play an outstanding role in policy making. In addition, differing perspectives from economic thinking are presented on behalf of their insightful perspectives about the challenges for enhancing competition and price stability. In this attempt, Alfred Marshall, Joan Robinson and Milton Friedman's contributions are considered.

Some topics on theories of economic growth and business cycles are structured around great debates that have present in capitalist societies over the past 300 years. In this attempt, we include the contributions of Adam Smith, Joseph Schumpeter and Hyman Minsky around the outcomes of free markets, the role of technology and entrepreneurship and the impacts of the financial set-up on economic growth and cyclical business dynamics. In addition, controversies around the best way to organize economic activity—through government, through free markets or some combination of the two – have been always present in the economic debates. These issues are addressed by considering the writings of David Ricardo, John Maynard Keynes and Friedrich von Hayek - economists whose contributions to the economic policy debate have been outstanding in real-world economics.

Finally, as concerns on welfare, justice and fairness have been closely intertwined in economic thought, we address these relevant topics by including the contributions of Arthur Pigou, Amartya Sen and Elinor Ostrom.

We believe that the eBook will provide a space for reflection about economic issues that arise whenever one seeks to understand the complex process of evolution of the capitalist system.

The systematic study of some of the most influential interpretations about the economic features and outcomes of the capitalist system certainly offers an excellent opportunity for humanists to deal with some of the central concerns of social scientists.

Maria Alejandra Madi
World Economics Association,
State University of Campinas,
Av. Angélica 1711, cj. 111,
São Paulo, SP,
Brazil
E-mail: alejandra_madi@yahoo.com.br

CONFLICT OF INTEREST

The author confirms that this book content has no conflict of interest.

ACKNOWLEDGEMENTS

The author is thankful to the anonymous referees whose recommendations enhanced achieve substantial improvements in the final edition.

"The study of economics does not seem to require any specialized gifts of an unusually high order. Is it not, intellectually regarded, a very easy subject compared with the higher branches of philosophy and pure science? Yet good, or even competent, economists are the rarest of birds. An easy subject at which very few excel! The paradox finds its explanation, perhaps, in that the master-economist must possess a rare combination of gifts. He must reach a high standard in several different directions and must combine talents not often found together. He must be mathematician, historian, statesman, philosopher - in some degree. He must understand symbols and speak in words. He must contemplate the particular in terms of the general, and touch abstract and concrete in the same flight of thought. He must study the present in the light of the past for the purposes of the future. No part of man's nature or his institutions must lie entirely outside his regard. He must be purposeful and disinterested in a simultaneous mood; as aloof and incorruptible as an artist, yet sometimes as near the earth as a politician".

(Keynes, Collected Writings, vol. X: Essays in Biography)

Economics: Current and Future Developments

Volume # 2

Pluralist Readings in Economics: Key concepts and policy tools for the 21st century

Author: Maria Alejandra Madi

ISSN (Online): 2452-2090

ISSN (Print): 2452-2082

ISBN (Online): 978-1-68108-506-7

ISBN (Print): 978-1-68108-507-4

CHAPTER 1

Evolution of Capitalism

Abstract: This chapter presents three critical appreciations about the capitalist system since the First Industrial Revolution in Britain until current globalization. Firstly, we consider Karl Polanyi's contribution about the First Industrial Revolution's effects on economic and social life. Then, we address the contribution of Rudolf Hilferding whose studies on financial capital highlights the role of banks in the expansion of large corporations and capital markets in the early 1900s. Finally, we consider Eric Hobsbawm's ideas about contemporary globalization that intertwines economic and political challenges along with social and cultural outcomes.

Keywords: First industrial revolution, Financial capital, Globalization.

1. INTRODUCTION

At the heart of modern economic thought lies an ongoing debate about the main features and the outcomes of the capitalist system. Which social, political, and moral relations emerge alongside the evolution of a capitalist economy? How are we to understand the larger historical significance of the financial transformations throughout the world? How has globalization transformed the world in which we live?

This chapter presents three critical appreciations about the capitalist system since the First Industrial Revolution in Britain until current globalization. First, we present Karl Polanyi's contribution about the First Industrial Revolution's decisive effects on economic life. He turned out to be world known on behalf of his criticism of the self-regulated markets as a "natural" institutional set-up where the search of individual enrichment is the "natural" characteristic of men.

Second, we address the contribution of Rudolf Hilferding who analyse the role of financial capital in the expansion of banks, large corporations and capital markets in the early 1900s. For him, the key to understanding the economic changes was the transition from free competition to monopoly. Indeed, Hilferding shows how the interconnections between banks and non–financial corporations create monopolies and cartels with market power to influence levels of output, prices and working conditions in different economic sectors.

Maria Alejandra Madi

Finally, we consider Eric Hobsbawm's interpretation about contemporary world history. He explored the economic and political challenges of globalization along with the cultural and social outcomes. Besides, he pointed out the threats to economic stability and peace at the beginning of 21st century.

1.1. Karl Polanyi on the Liberal Myth

1.1.1. Setting the Scene

Karl Paul Polanyi was critical of the methodological individualism of the Austrian school as the point of departure of economic analysis. His critique focused the assumption of *homo economicus* – the representation of the self-interested agent who maximizes utility in his choices. In the book *Trade and Markets in the Early Empires* (1957), he addresses that it is necessary to distinguish between the formal and the substantive meanings of the concept of 'economics'. Reflecting on the epistemological concerns that arise in Economics as a scientific knowledge, Polanyi states that, at his time, Economics as a discipline mainly depended on deductive methods of inquiry.

However, in Polanyi's view, the economic analysis must cope with multiple issues associated with human nature and human needs [1]. Polanyi invites us to re-examine the concept of economics as many people are accustomed to think that the only way of organizing men's livelihoods is the market economy. Indeed, in the introduction to *Trade and Markets,* he proposes a new theoretical construction in order to explain the place and role of human beings in the social and economic system. And he addresses that men value material goods only as these goods serve the promotion of social standing. Adopting the method of economic anthropology, Polanyi privileges the study of principles of economic behaviour that are induced from empirical observation. In this approach, the economic question becomes an anthropological question. And the study of Economics could be known as substantial.

In fact, the fundamental problem in economics, for Polanyi, is the attendance of human needs. Thus, the Polanyian concept of economics certainly offers to us a new way of looking at the "human beings" and at the "real economy" around us. This concept of economics is supported by ethical principles that touch on social justice. While taking into account different ways of organizing men's livelihoods, Polanyi provides a guide that stimulates empirical observations of economic life in the real world.

His criticism also focused on the myth of the self-regulated markets in capitalism. With the advance of industrialization, the liberal economic theory spread out the statement that the search of individual enrichment is the "natural" characteristic of men. For Polanyi, the institutional set-up and its economic and social outcomes cannot be considered "natural". Indeed, he looked for evidences in history and anthropology to show that the expansion and dominance of the behaviours based on the "economic motive" in the markets is essentially a modern phenomenon. The spread of this behaviour fosters the rupture of traditional social relations overwhelmed by links of reciprocity and redistribution within families and neighbourhoods.

The world-known Polanyi's book *The Great Transformation* (1944) emphasizes the deep impacts of industrialization on economic, social and cultural life. Indeed, Polanyi highlights the role of the free-market ideology in shaping a "new discipline" that supports the expansion of economic liberalism. The economic changes that enhanced and resulted from the Industrial Revolution cannot be apprehended if ignoring political, social and ethical issues. As one of the most original interpreters of the market economy, his analysis serves as an effective counter argument to free market fundamentalism.

Box 1. A biographical note.

Karl Polanyi was born in the city of Vienna in the year of 1886. While living in Budapest, he developed studies in Law and Philosophy.
In the 1920s, Polanyi worked as foreign editor of the Austrian leading economic publication *Österreichische Volkswirt*. On behalf of the European political crisis, he moved to England and then, in 1940, he accepted the invitation to give lectures in the United States. When he was working at Bennington College in Vermont, Polany concluded his book The *Great Transformation* that was first published in 1944. His academic career included a Visiting Professorship at Columbia University between 1947 and 1953. After his retirement, he continued to develop research projects while partly living in the U.S. and in Canada. Concerned with the stability of the world peace, he founded an international journal related to comparative studies of economics and politics. The first issue of the journal *Co-existence* was published in the year of his death, 1964 [2].

Box 2. Selected works.

Books
1937. Christianity and the Social Revolution.
1944. The Great Transformation: The Political and Economic Origins of Our Time
1957. Trade and Markets in the Early Empires. Economies in History and Theory
1963. The Plough and the Pen. Writings from Hungary, 1930-1956
1977. The Livelihood of Man.
Collected essays
1966. Dahomey and the Slave Trade. An Analysis of an Archaic Economy
1968. Primitive, Archaic, and Modern Economies: Essays of Karl Polanyi

1.1.2. Key Concepts

When reading Karl Polanyi, you must remember that:

1. In the context of capitalism as a market society, livelihoods are embedded in the economic setting rather than the economic dynamics embedded in social life. This happens because the economic motive overwhelms social life.
2. Throughout the First Industrial Revolution, economic, social and cultural transformations turned out to subordinate social relations to the market economy. The economic changes that resulted from the Industrial Revolution cannot be apprehended if ignoring the political, social and ethical issues.
3. The commodity fiction is the vital organizing process in the market economy: the main commodities are labour, land and money.
4. Through the evolution of capitalism, the double movement refers both to the creation of the market economy institutional set up and to the emergence of mechanisms of social protection to face the harmful social effects of the capitalist economic system.

1.1.3. Reading Passages: The Great Transformation

The Reading Passages presented below were written by Karl Polanyi and were published in the book *The Great Transformation: The Political and Economic Origins of Our Time,* 1944 [3]. In order to have in-depth understanding of Polanyi's contribution, we elaborated a summary of the main ideas.

Reading Passages	***Summary of the Main Ideas***
Before the process had advanced very far, the labouring people had been crowded together in new places of desolation, the so-called industrial towns of England; the country folk had been dehumanized into slum dwellers; the family was on the road to perdition; and large parts of the country were rapidly disappearing under the slack and scrap heaps vomited forth from the "satanic mills." Writers of all views and parties, conservatives and liberals, capitalists and socialists invariably referred to social conditions under the Industrial Revolution as a veritable abyss of human degradation.	*The Great Transformation underlines that the process of social change created by trade and industrialization led to the emergence of poverty on a large scale. The desolation, dehumanization and degradation of human lives were necessary steps for the emergence of a labour market.*
A market economy is an economic system controlled, regulated, and directed by markets alone; order in the production and distribution of goods is entrusted to this self-regulating mechanism. An economy of this kind derives from the expectation that human beings behave in such a way as to achieve maximum money gains.... Self-regulation implies that all production is for sale on the market and that all incomes derive from such sales. Accordingly, there are markets for all elements of industry, not only for goods (always including services) but also for labour, land and money, their prices being called respectively commodity prices, wages, rent, and interest.	*In the market economy, labour, land and money turn out to be seen as commodities for sale.*

Contd.....

Reading Passages	*Summary of the Main Ideas*
Nevertheless, it is with the help of this fiction that the actual markets for labour, land, and money are organized; they are being actually bought and sold on the market. Now, in regard to labour, land, and money such a postulate cannot be upheld. … (if land is treated as a commodity then) … Nature would be reduced to its elements, neighborhoods and landscapes defiled, rivers polluted, military safety jeopardized, the power to produce food and raw materials destroyed. Finally, the market administration of purchasing power would periodically liquidate business enterprise, for shortages and surfeits of money would prove as disastrous to business as floods and droughts in primitive society.	*The commodity fiction is a vital organizing process. Labour, land and money turn out to be seen as fictitious commodities bought and sold in the market. Within the market society the social relations are embedded in the economy rather than the economy embedded in social relations.*
The true significance of the tormenting problem of poverty now stood revealed: economic society was subjected to laws which were not human laws.	*The laws governing a market competitive society are not human laws.*
The action of two organizing principles in society, each of them set special institutional aims, having the support of definite social forces and using its own distinctive methods. The one was the principle of economic liberalism, aiming at the establishment of a self-regulating market …; the other was the principle of social protection aiming at the conservation of man and nature as well as productive organization.	*The historical evolution of capitalism has always been followed by the sprouting of safeguards to protect society against the interference of the market practices.*
Economic liberalism was the organizing principle of a society engaged in creating a market system. Born as a mere penchant for nonbureaucratic methods, it evolved into a veritable faith in man's secular salvation through a self-regulating market. Such fanaticism was the result of the sudden aggravation of the task it found itself committed to: the magnitude of the sufferings that were to be inflicted on innocent persons as well as the vast scope of the interlocking changes involved in the establishment of the new order. The liberal creed assumed its evangelical fervor only in response to the needs of a fully deployed market economy.	*The ideology of the free markets supports the spread of economic liberalism.*

1.1.4. Modern Concerns About Free Market Fundamentalism

Karl Polanyi's contribution to the economic and social analysis of the origin of capitalism motivates a reflection about the social outcomes of neoliberal policies. In *The Great Transformation*, Polanyi highlighted both the critique of the myth of liberalism and the challenges to promote economic and social justice, showing that the dehumanization of capitalism is the result of the institutional features of the market society. Taking into account the historical and institutional analysis of capitalism enhanced by Polanyi, an outstanding idea to consider, in any ethically defensible approach to inequality, is that the institutional patterns adjust perfectly to the principles of behaviour in society [4].

The systemic and institutional approach to capitalism presented by Polanyi adds fruitful ideas to expand our understanding of current social challenges. Since the late 1970s, the evolution of disembedded capitalism enhanced a global pattern of accumulation that turned out to enlarge social exclusion. In this setting, institutional changes have been promoted by nation-states to deep financial and trade liberalization and the flexibilization of all markets. As a result, the expansion of the profit motive and the global commodification of money have created new economic and political pressures that foster the dissolution of reciprocity interrelations. Indeed, the mode of expansion of the capitalist capitalism in the 21st century -overwhelmed by the financialization of wealth and social exclusion- is far from being "natural" [5].

Taking into account the social challenges, David Weil's 2014 book *The Fissured Workplace* highlights that today the employer-worker relationship has been submitted to delivering value to investors [6]. As Weil's shows, the result has been an ever-widening income inequality. According to the Global Labour Union IUF, the current global business models foster deleterious conditions in the workplace, more control of workers, decreasing employment stability and a lower formalization rate of employment. Today, informal unemployment includes self-employment in small unregistered enterprises, unpaid workers, own account operators and also unpaid work in family businesses. As a result, the total amount of informal workers also includes: day workers, home workers and workers occupied in the context of outsourcing agreements.

In short, the evidences related to the recent economic and social disruptions serve as an effective counter-argument to free market fundamentalism.

1.1.5. Further Reading

1. Block, F., & Somers, M. R. (2014). *The Power of Market Fundamentalism: Karl Polanyi's critique.* Cambridge, MA and London, England.
2. Bugra, A., & Agartan, K. (Eds.) (2007). *Market Economy as a Political Project: Reading Karl Polanyi for the 21st Century.* Basingstoke: Palgrave.
3. Dale, G. (2010). *Karl Polanyi: The Limits of the Market.* Cambridge: Polity Press.
4. McRobbie, K. (Ed.) (1994) *Humanity, Society and Commitment: On Karl Polanyi.* Montreal: Black Rose Books.
5. McRobbie, K., & Polanyi-Levitt, K. (Eds.) (2000.*) Karl Polanyi in Vienna: The Contemporary Significance of the Great Transformation.* Montreal: Black Rose Books
6. Mendell, M., & Salée, D. (1991). *The Legacy of Karl Polanyi: Market, State, and Society at the End of the Twentieth Century.* New York: St. Martin's Press.
7. Polanyi-Levitt, K. (Ed.) (1990). *The Life and Work of Karl Polany.,* Montreal: Black Rose Books.

8. Stanfield, J. R. (1986). *The Economic Thought of Karl Polanyi: Lives and Livelihood.* New York: St. Martin's Press.

1.2. Rudolf Hilferding on Financial Capital

1.2.1. Setting the Scene

It was in 1910 that Rudolf Hilferding - a young Austrian physician interested in economics - published the book *Finanz Kapital* that aims to analyse the then-current capitalist development. Based on the dynamics of the German banking model, his contribution presents a deep analysis of the institutional set up of financial relations and power bloc features. Proceeding from Marx´s approach to the study of capitalism, Hilferding deepens the analyses on central banks, banks´ strategies, capital markets, commodity markets, monopolization and regulation of competition.

Box 3. A biographical note.

Rudolf Hilferding was born in 1877 in Vienna, Austria. He became attracted to socialism while studying medicine. Prior to World War I, he became a teacher in the German Social Democratic Party.
Hilferding served as Weimar finance minister in 1923 in the context of a highly inflationary process. In the period between 1928 and 1930, he served at the Mueller cabinet in a context of economic depression [7].
After Hitler came to power, Hilferding went to France and continued the struggle against Nazism. However, in 1940, he was arrested by the Vichy authorities and was sent to the Gestapo.
Before dying in a German prison cell in 1941, Hilferding was a leading economic thinker, besides a prominent socialist theorist and politician. Indeed, his democratic attempts to strengthen republican and socialist ideas in confrontation with the outcomes of Nazism and communism [8].

Box 4. Selected works.

Articles
1905. Parliamentarianism and the General Strike
1933. Between Decisions
1940. State Capitalism or Totalitarian State Economy
Books
1904. Böhm-Bawerk's Criticism of Marx
1910. Finance Capital: A Study of the Latest Phase of Capitalist Development

Credit money enhances the development of the stock markets and the monopolization of industries. Hilferding emphasizes the importance of banks and credit operations in fostering the growth of large-scale corporations that are organized as joint-stock companies. In these companies, the separation of ownership and control reinforces changes in management. The evolving interactions between the banking system and large-scale monopolistic industries lead to the definition of new banks´ strategies that turn out to deepen the control of corporations through fictitious capital (securities, shares). Following these economic transformations, industrial capitalism was replaced by financial capitalism where centralized and liquid capital subordinates the path of economic growth.

In the early 1900s, the new financial oligarchy did not only dominate the financial operations of the economy, but also subordinated the whole economic and social dynamics. The relations between this oligarchy and the nation-states reveal the interactions between the economic and political powers. In this setting, although industrialization was considered a period of massive technological innovations and rapid expansion, the huge productivity increases in manufacturing did not improve the living conditions of the working classes.

1.2.2. Key Concepts

When reading Rudolf Hilferding, you must remember that:

1. Britain's international role in the world began to erode, even though it still remained important as an international trade and banker after the Second Industrial Revolution. This new historical phase is called as Monopolist Capitalism since the real-world economy is characterized by the capital concentration in industrial markets that is leveraged by financial institutions. The new trends express the transformation of business under the dominance of centralized and liquid capital.
2. Financial capital reveals the inherent tendency of capitalist accumulation towards the predominance of interest-bearing capital.
3. Financial capital expands with the growth of joint-stock corporations that fosters industrial monopolization.
4. In the context of the monopolization of industry, large banks increasingly expand their power over business and fictitious capital.

1.2.3. Reading Passages: Finance Capital

The Reading Passages presented below were written by Rudolf Hilferding and were published in the book *Finance Capital: A Study of the Latest Phase of Capitalist Development,* 1910 [9]. In order to have in-depth understanding of Hilferding's contribution, we elaborated a summary of the main ideas.

Reading Passages	***Summary of the Main Ideas***
Banks become the institutions for clearing and settling balances, a technical improvement which extends the range of possible mutual cancellation and reduces the amount of cash required for settling balances. The money which productive capitalists had previously been obliged to keep on hand for settling the bills they had drawn now becomes superfluous, and flows as deposits to the banks who can use it to settle the balances.	*The relationship between banks and productive capitalists turns to be closer.*

Contd.....

Reading Passages	*Summary of the Main Ideas*
The professional banking principle of maximum security makes the banks inherently averse to competition, and predisposed in favour of the elimination of competition in industry through cartels, and its replacement by a 'steady profit'.	*Banks are active agents in the process of monopolization.*
The trust has an advantage over the cartel in fixing prices. The cartel is obliged to base its fixed price on the price of production of the most expensive producer among its member firms, whereas for the trust there is only one uniform price of production in which the costs of the more efficient and less efficient concerns are averaged out. The trust can set a price which allows it to maximize its output and make up for its small profit per unit by the volume of its turnover. Furthermore, the trust can close down the less profitable concerns much more easily than can the cartel. When production has to be cut down, the trust can effect this exclusively in the high-cost enterprises, and thus reduce average costs of production; and conversely, when there is an expansion of production it can concentrate the increase in the technically more efficient firms. As a rule, the cartel has to distribute the increased production evenly among its member enterprises. In this way, the technically superior enterprises gain, from the prices fixed by the cartel, extra profits which are not averaged out through competition, since the cartel excludes this, and seem to assume the character of a differential rent.	*Trusts and cartels have different strategies to reduce the competition in the markets.*
The development of capitalist industry produces concentration of banking, and this concentrated banking system is itself an important force in attaining the highest stage of capitalist concentration in cartels and trusts.	*The concentration of the banking system enhances the expansion of cartels and trusts.*
Finance capital develops with the development of the joint-stock company and reaches its peak with the monopolization of industry. Industrial earnings acquire a more secure and regular character, and so the possibilities for investing bank capital in industry are extended. But the bank disposes of bank capital, and the owners of the majority of the shares in the bank dominate the bank. It is clear that with the increasing concentration of property, the owners of the fictitious capital which gives power over the banks, and the owners of the capital which gives power over industry, become increasingly the same people. As we have seen, this is all the more so as the large banks increasingly acquire the power to dispose over fictitious capital.	*The expansion of join-stock companies is crucial for the expansion of fictitious capital and speculation. Finance capital and the monopolization of the economy are inter-related processes.*

1.2.4. Modern Concerns About Financialization and Speculation

The outcomes of the 1930 Great Depression and subsequent financial regulation devastated the power of financial capital. However, after the 1970s, great transformations in the relations between governments, banks, non-banks, investors and managers shaped the financialization of the capitalist economy.

Financialization has been characterized as the long-run process of financial expansion where monopoly-finance capital turned out to become increasingly dependent on credit and financial bubbles [10]. This process of financialization of the global economy, that was initiated at the end of the 1970s and intensified after the 1990s, produced great transformations in the growth patterns after World War II [11]. Increasing subordination of business to the financial commitment to short-term profits has revealed, as Hilferding warned, that financial capital shapes the market dynamics and enhances speculative decisions.

Indeed, looking back, between 1945 and 1971, the U.S. surplus was at the centre of the global economic order. Throughout the Bretton Woods period, the U.S. exported goods to the rest of the world and also finance these purchases. From the 1950s to the 70s, The United States recycled its surpluses *via* foreign direct investment in Germany (and also Japan). Indeed, the United States was the country which recycled part of its surplus in Western Europe and Japan. Thus, the U.S. created demand for its own exports, but also for the exports of Western countries, primarily Germany and Japan.

After the 1970s, this system of international flows changed. From 1971 to 2008, there is the expansion of the age of high finance where the US deficits were at the centre of the global economic order. In the 2013 book *The Global Minotaur: America, Europe and the Future of the Global Economy,* what the Greek economist Yanis Varoufakis calls the “Global Minotaur” is a system of international economic flows, according to which the whole world surpluses financed the unsustainable expansion of a double deficit on which the U.S. has built its political and economic hegemony [12]. The U.S. formed increasing deficit in the current account, along with a government budget deficit, in the “Global Minotaur era”.

In this setting, without Wall Street institutions recycling the global surpluses, the U.S. had not been able to hold its twin deficits. Indeed, the new global order after the 1970s was supported thanks to the close collaboration of high finance and its political power in neo-liberalism. In this scenario, the global expansion of corporations and supply chains enhanced business models based on increasingly lower wages. As a result, the global surplus recycling mechanisms reversed the flow of global trade and capital flows: the U.S. provided sufficient demand for manufacturing in foreign countries - mainly in China - in return for capital inflows. As a matter of fact, between 1971 and 2008, the era of high finance supported the expansion of global trade at the cost of financial bubbles, corporate mega-profits and increasing social inequalities.

Consequently, in the period between 1992 and 2006, the American credit expansion, with rising banks’ net interest income and low credit losses, was the major driver of financial fragility. Banks managed capital requirements adjusted to risk in order to expand credit. As a result, they were interested in selling loans so as to also manage credit and liquidity risks. Taking into account the U.S. experience, financial fragility spread to the large American investment banks that were not subject to prudential supervision. In truth, both commercial and investment banks held a great number of "toxic" securities on their balance sheets. Soon after the crisis, these institutions proved to out of funding to face their liabilities. The lack of liquidity spread to markets for credit-default swaps, for *structured securities* and even for U.S. Treasuries. As a result, restricted demand for these assets negatively affected their yields. In this scenario, the threatening of systemic risk was founded on the deep global interconnection between the financial markets and the lack of information about banks' exposures.

If we look at the American downturn in terms of the lessons learned, the outstanding features of this crisis result from structural changes imposed by financial liberalization. The recent American financial crisis is an example of how financial institutions encouraged speculation dependent on future housing prices, the future price of securitized assets and the renewal of lending operations. American banks have turned out to encourage speculative operations that depended on the future prices of houses, future prices of the securitized assets and the renewals of the lending operations. In this scenario, low interest rates supported an environment of low capital costs.

The global financial crisis has revealed lasting impacts on the world economy and, above all, on banks. Losses from subprime mortgage investments, conventional credit losses, loss of market capitalization, lack of capital, among other features, shape the current challenges. While American banks have been at the heart of the problem, the evolution of many domestic financial systems has revealed the deeply interconnected features of credit and capital markets in the context of financialization.

The "Global Minotaur" had a crucial weakness. Indeed, the last cause of the global crisis is founded on the Minotaur's dynamics that were synonymous to the global asymmetries on which the global architecture was built after the 1970s. Indeed, the American supremacy requires global permanent unbalances. In short, the global surplus recycling mechanism could not stabilize the world economy.

As the fundamental structural flaws in the global economy have not been addressed, there are serious concerns that a global economic crisis of unprecedented magnitude could still happen.

1.2.5. Further Reading

1. Coakley, J. (1994). Hilferding's Finance Capital. *Capital and Class*, 17,

134–141.
2. Coakley, J. (2000). "Hilferding, Rudolf" In P. Arestis & P. Sawyer (Eds.) *A Biographical Dictionary of Dissenting Economists.* Cheltenham: Edward Elgar, 290-298.
3. Howard, M. C., & King, J. (2003). Rudolf Hilferding, In W.J. Samuels (Ed.) *European Economists of the Early 20th Century* (Vol. II, 119-135). Cheltenham: Edward Elgar.
4. Smaldone, W. (1998). *Rudolf Hilferding: The Tragedy of a German Social Democrat.* Dekalb:Northern Illinois University Press
5. Wagner, E. P. (1996). Rudolf *Hilferding: Theory and Politics of Democratic Socialism.* New Jersey: Atlantic Highlands Humanities Press.
6. Zoninsein, J. (1990). *Monopoly Capital Theory: Hilferding and Twentieh-Century Capitalism.* New York: Greenwood Press.
7. Zoninsein, J. (2000). Rudolf Hilferding´s theory of finance capitalism and today's world financial markets. In P. Koslowski (Ed.) *The Theory of Capitalism in the German Economic Tradition* (275-304). Berlin and Heidelberg: Springer Verlag.

1.3. Eric Hobsbawn on Globalisation

1.3.1. Setting the Scene

Eric Hobsbawm, a contemporary well-known historian, in his 2007 book *Globalisation, Democracy and Terrorism,* underlines both the complex outcomes of the global free markets' dynamics and the difficulties of nation-states to guarantee public order within their frontiers [13]. Market liberalization has also been a period of growing inequality, both within and across countries, along with increasing unemployment, informal labour and changes in pensions.

Hobsbawm analyses the very real facts of globalization and shows its economic, social and political limits in historical perspective. He contrasts the American imperialism with the British Empire and shows how the U.S. power has been in decline.

In his view, there is a profound crisis of authority within nation-states. In particular, national democracies have to face global problems, not only climate change, but notably the transnational nature of global investment and its effects on policy making and social dynamics. In this scenario, violence, civil conflicts and terrorism threaten public order and individual freedom.

Mainly since September 2001, the increasing control over individuals and the transformations of political violence in a "war against terror" have also revealed endemic manifestations of the deep economic and social imbalances historically built throughout the last decade at global and local levels.

Box 5. A biographical note.

Eric John Ernest Hobsbawm was born in the city of Alexandria, Egypt, in 1917. After the death of his father in 1929, he moved from Viena to Berlin and then to London with his uncle.
Hobsbawm studied at the St. Marylebone Grammar School and he got his bachelor's degree at King's College, Cambridge, in 1939. In 1947, he joined Birkbeck, University of London, as a lecturer in History where he remained at the end of his life. He became Professor in 1970, Emeritus Professor of History in 1982 and President of the college in 2002. His first academic work called *Labour's Turning Point* was published in 1948.
He participated in the Historians' Group of the British Communist Party, among other important intellectuals such as Christopher Hill, E. P. Thompson, John Saville, Rodney Hilton, George Rudé, Victor Kiernan. Besides, Hobsbawm was one of the founders of the journal *Past and Present* in 1952. After the 1960s, besides his interest in political movements, he wrote essays and books about contemporary issues in historical perspective [14].
Hobsbawm died in 2012, at the age of 95.

Box 6. Selected works.

Books
1959. Primitive Rebels. Studies in Archaic Forms of Social Movement in the 19th and 20th centuries
1962. The Age of Revolution: Europe, 1789-1848
1975. The Age of Capital: 1848-1875
1989. The Age of Empire: 1875-1914
1990. Nations and Nationalism since 1780,
1994. The Age of extremes. The short twentieth century 1914-1991
2002. Interesting Times: A Twentieth-Century life
2007. Globalisation, Democracy and Terrorism
2011. How to Change the World: Tales of Marx and Marxism
2013. Fractured Times: Culture and Society in the 20th Century

Consequently, Hobsbawm highlights that contemporary global political and economic dynamics threaten individual freedom and put pressure on the control on social life. The transformation of political violence reveals the overall changes in the economy and society where a lengthy process of deregulation has been privileged. Among his concerns on livelihoods at the beginning of the 21st century, he addresses that our century is a period of fear, insecurity and barbarization where peace is far from being a reality.

1.3.2. Key Concepts

When reading Eric Hobsbawm, you must remember that:

1. In the nineteenth century, the Pax Britannica was a period associated with the hegemony of the British Empire. During this period, there was a classic

division of economic activities between industrialized central countries and the peripheral countries that produce food and raw materials. In this setting, the British economy was a driver of the world economy's growth. In the 1880s, Britain consumed almost half of the world-wide traded wheat and meat and bought most of the tea and raw cotton, besides 35% of the wood.

2. Throughout the Second Industrial Revolution, the control over the international markets was redefined. This period of national rivalries and neocolonialism expressed the conflicts that arose from the reorganization of manufacturing and trade flows at the system level.
3. In the mid-1950s, the American hegemony changed the world order. After World War II, a redefinition of international trade agreements favoured a gradual liberalization of international trade flows. Throughout this period, American corporations enhanced inter and intra-firm international trade flows. There was a generalization of the American growth model's main features: industrialization, urbanization, mass consumption, cheap energy (oil). Within this setting, development strategies were linked to the coordination of economic policies to foster growth by nation–states.
4. After the 1970s, the influence of globalization over economic, social, cultural and political life has spread huge challenges, including weak economic growth, higher income inequality, violence, civil conflicts and wars in a context where nation-states seem to be unable to face social needs and the maintenance of public order.

1.3.3. Reading Passages: Globalisation, Democracy and Terrorism

The Reading Passages presented below were written by Eric Hobsbawm and were published in the book *Globalisation, Democracy and Terrorism,* 2007 [15]. In order to have in-depth understanding of Hobsbawn's contribution, we elaborated a summary of the main ideas.

Reading Passages	***Summary of the Main Ideas***
(…) the twenty- first century is not likely to be as murderous as it was in the twentieth. But armed violence, creating disproportionate suffering and loss, will remain omnipresent and endemic – occasionally epidemic- in a large part of the world. The prospect of a century of peace is remote.	*Although resisting to express opinions on the future, Hobsbawm presents a pessimistic view of the world's future*
We have a rapidly globalizing world economy based on transnational private firms that are doing their best to live outside the range of state law and taxes, which severely limits the ability of even big governments to control their national economies. Indeed, thanks to the prevailing theology of the free market, states are actually abandoning many of their most traditional direct activities –postal services, police, prisons, even vital parts of the armed forces- to profit-making private contractors.	*In the context of globalization, the redefinition and reorientation of the scope of the state actions have re-shaped the relations between the state and the capitalist private firms.*

Contd.....

Reading Passages	*Summary of the Main Ideas*
The only effective actors are states.	*The challenges to the contemporary scenario of instability and inequalities reveal that the world increasingly seems to require supranational solutions to supranational or transnational problems. Nevertheless, there is no global authority to assume these political decisions. Neither the World Bank, nor the International Monetary Fund, or even the World Trade Organization is able to do this.*
Participation in the market replaces participation in politics; the consumer takes the place of the citizen.	*The current phase of globalized capitalist development is undermining the basis of popular governments, including the liberal-democratic ones.*
They seem to reflect the profound social dislocations brought about at all levels of society by the most rapid and dramatic transformation in human life and society experienced within single lifetimes. They also seem to reflect both a crisis in traditional systems of authority, hegemony and legitimacy in the west and their breakdown in the east and the south, as well as a crisis in the traditional movements that claimed to provide an alternative to these.	*Recent evidences reinforced the menaces to social cohesion and justice in current capitalist societies*

1.3.4. Modern Concerns About the Neo-liberal Agenda

Since the 1970s, the legitimization of the neo-liberal agenda favoured the advance of market deregulation that turned out to be a set of recommendations toward global economic integration. In this setting, the "good" global governance agenda -supported by multilateral financial institutions- promoted the relevance of free markets and private agents to improve efficiency, competitiveness and growth in a macroeconomic context of price stability. As a result, economic and social differences across countries could be attributed to institutions and policies that determine the environment where economic agents accumulate abilities and firms accumulate capital, invest in technology and generate income [16].

As Hobsbawm suggested, neo-liberalism and globalization seem to have become inseparable concepts and, over the last couple of decades, their outcomes had provoked undeniable effects on societies all around the world. The outcomes of the macroeconomic stabilization and structural reforms toward market flexibility were conditioned by the local institutional set-up that was built in the Bretton Woods period.

Indeed, the adoption of the neo-liberal agenda turned out to foster the reorganization of economic and social life under the dominance of financial capital. New patterns of interactions between domestic and foreign economic sectors have been established in a global context where the behaviour of transnational corporations and investors shape governments' targets and policy options [17]. Besides, new capitalist production conditions have revealed the reorganization of markets into global production chains where flexibility in employment rights and work organization have been overwhelmed by macroeconomic instability and new financial systemic risks. In the allocation of public resources, the criteria of efficiency have subordinated equity and social justice.

1.3.5. Further Reading

1. Cronin, J. (1979). Creating a Marxist Historiography: the contribution of Hobsbawm. *Radical History Review*, 19, 87–109.
2. Cronin, J. M. (2003). Social History and Commitment: Eric Hobsbawm's Interesting Times. *Journal of Social History*, 37 (1), 219-231.
3. Elliott, G. (2010). *Hobsbawm: History and Politics*, London: Pluto Press.
4. Samuel, R., & Jones, G. S. (Eds.) (1982). *Culture, Ideology and Politics: essays for Eric Hobsbawm.* London: Routledge & Kegan Paul.
5. Snowman, D. (1999). Eric Hobsbawm. *History Today*, 49 (1), 16–18.
6. Thane, P., Crossick, G., & Floud, R. (Eds.) (1984). *The Power of the Past: essays for Eric Hobsbawm.* Cambridge: Cambridge University Press.
7. Wrigley, C. (1984). Eric Hobsbawm: an appreciation. *Bulletin of the Society for the Study of Labour History*, 38 (1), 2.

1.4. Policy tools: Government-led Corporate Social Responsibility Initiatives

In the last decades, the debate about the importance of an efficient corporate governance system has gained importance between investors and corporations. This fact has been related to the growing needs of news forms of financing, as good practices of corporate governance are aimed to overcome asymmetric information and structure efficient systems of financial leverage, and on another side, to the growing demand of transparency by investors.

Considering this setting, corporate social responsibility (CSR) involves the adoption of voluntary global values to create new practices in business culture in order to modify the relationship among corporations, employees, clients, suppliers, communities and governments. Small businesses are also part of this setting.

In the corporate sector, CSR is about managing change forms of social protection in a globalized market system. The CSR practices, at the heart of long-run value creation, should reveal the commitment to transparent information to shareholders; quality of goods and services and decent labour conditions.

The CRS guidelines reinforce the integration of the corporations into local communities in order to promote social projects with emphasis on sustainability. In this context, corporate decisions need to express social responsibility, sharing with governments, clients, suppliers and employees the achievement of the goal of economic sustainability.

The multilateral organizations' attempts to highlight the relevance of adopting better business practices have also revealed the global concern about relevant issues, such as discrimination, child and forced labour, in addition to freedom of association and collective bargaining. In this respect, the United Nations Global Compact's labour principles – also defended by the International Labour Organization (ILO) - provide guidance and support to address these issues [18]. The general idea is that management strategies, while searching a balanced relation among profit, workers and natural resources, would lead to inclusive economic growth.

So far the decisive question is: which should be the guidelines to foster CSR practices in current business?

A wide range of government-led CSR initiatives can be identified from awareness-raising and promotional to legislative actions. To encourage business organizations to address their commitment to society, public support to self- and co-regulation processes has been improved. For instance, in Spain, awareness-raising and promotional policies have been adopted. 100 measures have been implemented to support youth employment as part of Spain's comprehensive public program named *Strategy for Entrepreneurship and Youth Employment* [19].

Private organizations or companies that participate in the implementation of the strategy's 100 measures should be committed to

- Carry out actions in the labour market for people under 25 years old;
- Conduct and/or support education and training for young people;
- Cooperate with public administrations.

REFERENCES

[1] Madi MA. The liberal myth: a critique 2013. Retrieved from: https://weapedagogy.wordpress.com/2013/07/10/the-liberal-myth-a-critique/

[2] Editors of the International Encyclopedia of the Social Sciences. Polanyi Karl. International Encyclopedia of the Social Sciences 2017. Retrieved from: http://www.encyclopedia.com

[3] Polanyi K. The Great Transformation: The Political and Economic Origins of Our Time. New York: Rinehart 1944.

[4] Madi MA, Gonçalves JR. Corporate social responsibility and market society: credit and banking inclusion in Brazil. In: Bugra A, Agartan K, Eds. Market Economy as a Political Project: Reading Karl Polanyi for the 21st Century.. Basingstoke: Palgrave 2007. [http://dx.doi.org/10.1057/9780230607187_13]

[5] Akyuz Y. Financial Liberalization: The Key Issues. Unctad Discussion Papers. 1993; 56.; Serfati C. Le rôle actif des groupes à domaine industrielle dans la financiarisation de l'économie. La Mondialisation Financière: Genèse, coût et enjeux. F. (Ed.)., Paris: Syros.: F. Chesnais 1996.; Toporowski J. The Economics and Culture of Financialisation, School of Oriental and African Studies, University of London, Department Of Economics Working Papers No158. London, UK 2008.

[6] Weil D. The Fissured Workplace: Why Work Became So Bad for So Many and What Can Be Done to Improve It. Cambridge, MA: Harvard University Press 2014. [http://dx.doi.org/10.4159/9780674726123]

[7] Editors of Encyclopædia Britannic. Rudolf Hilferding. International Encyclopedia of the Social Sciences 2017. https://global.britannica.com/biography/Rudolf-Hilferding

[8] Smaldone W. Rudolf Hilferding The Tragedy of a German Social Democrat. Dekalb: Northern Illinoies University Press 1998.

[9] Hilferding R. Finance Capital: A Study of the Latest Phase of Capitalist Development 1910. https://www.marxists.org/archive/hilferding/1910/finkap/

[10] Eichengreen B. *Globalizing Capital. A History of the International Monetary System*. Princeton, NJ: Princeton University Press. Foster, J. B. (2006). Monopoly-Finance Capital. Mon Rev 1996; 58: 7.

[11] Bello W. 2006. The capitalist conjuncture: Over-accumulation, financial crises, and the retreat from globalization. *Third World Quarterly*, 27(8), 1345–1367; Duménil, G. and Lévy, D. (2011). *The crisis of neoliberalism*. Cambridge, MA. Harvard University Press.

[12] Varoufakis Y. The Global Minotaur: America, Europe and the Future of the Global Economy, by Yanis Varoufakis. New York: Zed Books 2013.

[13] Gonçalves JR, Madi MA. Book Review: Globalisation, Democracy and Terrorism by Eric Hobsbawm. Int J of Green Economics 2009; 3(1): 103-6. [http://dx.doi.org/10.1504/IJGE.2009.026496]

[14] Blackbourn D. Memorial Eric John Ernest Hobsbawm, 1917–2012. Central European History Association 2013; 46 [http://dx.doi.org/10.1017/S0008938913000666]

[15] Hobsbawm E. Globalisation, Democracy and Terrorism. London: Abacus 2007.

[16] Madi MA, Gonçalves JR. Microcredit and market society: challenges to social inclusion in the 21st century. Conference Proceedings.

[17] Grabel I. The Political Economy of 'Policy Credibility': The New-Classical Macroeconomics and the Remaking of Emerging Economies. Camb J Econ 2000; 24: 1-19. [http://dx.doi.org/10.1093/cje/24.1.1]

[18] UN Global Compat. The Labour Principles of the UN Global Compact – A Guide for Business 2008. Retrieved from: https://www.unglobalcompact.org/docs/issues_doc/labour/the_labour_principles_a_guide_for_business.pdf

[19] Gobierno de España, Ministerio de Empleo y Seguridad Social. Strategy for Entrepreneurship and Youth Employment 2013-2016 Executive Summary 2012. Retrieved from: http://www.empleo.gob.es/ficheros/garantiajuvenil/documentos/EEEJ_Resumen_Ejecutivo_INGLES.pdf

CHAPTER 2

Capital, Labour and Power

Abstract: This chapter addresses the contributions of Karl Marx, Michal Kalecki and John Galbraith to these power issues. Firstly, we begin with Karl Marx who pointed out the centrality of class analysis to the study of power in capitalism. Then, we consider the analysis of Michal Kalecki on the degree of monopoly. Proceeding from a Marxist tradition, his analysis highlights important contemporary issues related to power in market structures and their outcomes in terms of income distribution. Finally, we present the main ideas of John Galbraith on the modern institutions. He deeply analysed the institutional set up of large corporations and highlighted their power in the markets and their relations with the nation-state.

Keywords: Capitalist system, Market power, Large corporations.

2. INTRODUCTION

Considering the power issues at stake in the capital accumulation process, relevant questions have emerged in the economic debate. Does capitalism promote freedom? Can it only provide the framework for one class to exploit another? Which are the relations within the capitalist class? Which is the role of the government?

This chapter addresses the contributions of Karl Marx, Michal Kalecki and John Galbraith to these power issues. First, we begin with Karl Marx who pointed out the centrality of class analysis to the study of power in capitalism. In this approach, the concept of class is a relational one and refers to the relation between those people that own the means of production and those who work for them.

Second, we consider the analysis of Michal Kalecki on the degree of monopoly. Proceeding from a Marxist tradition, Kalecki's analysis of the oligopolistic trends in contemporary capitalism highlights contemporary issues of power in market structures and their outcomes in terms of income distribution. His concern is to show how, in contemporary capitalism, income distribution between profits and wages are linked to the prices fixed in markets where corporate power is a reality.

Maria Alejandra Madi

Finally, we present the main ideas of John Galbraith on the modern institutions. He deeply analysed the institutional set up of large corporations and highlighted their power in the markets and their relations with the nation-state.

2.1. Karl Marx on Capital as a Social Relation

2.1.1. Setting the Scene

Proceeding from the German philosophic school, Karl Marx´s studies on political economy and the development of the historical materialist argument are relevant advances in economic knowledge in the 19th century.

In his earliest writings on political economy, capital refers to the stock of durable fixed capital, such as machinery, warehouses and factories. Indeed, Marx re-thought this concept to highlight the 'social relations of production'. In *A Contribution to the Critique of Political Economy* (1859) he states that livelihoods are conditioned by the main features of the economic production. And he adds that it is the social existence of men determines their consciousness.

Marx also highlights that social relations appear inverted as social relations between commodities in the dynamics of market exchanges. This idea refers to the concept of the 'fetishism of commodities' that he introduced in his famous book *Capital,* published in 1867.

Marx explains how capitalism, as a mode of production, replaces the production for subsistence by production for trade in the markets. Workers and capitalists as formally free individuals meet as commodity owners in the market. Marx addresses that the real subsumption of labour means the subordination of human beings to machinery in the capitalist mode of production. Indeed, he understood that in large scale capitalist production, the alienating effects of technology overwhelm the mechanization of labour and life under industrialization.

While living abroad in France and England, Karl Marx deeply understood the struggles of civil society. Power is concentrated in the hands of capitalists who use it to benefit themselves (increasing their rate of profit) while exploiting the workers. As the free workers own only their ability to work, they must work for the capitalists for a wage.

Marx uncovers the economic laws of motion of capitalism. While focusing on the phenomenon of commodity exchange, he shows how capital exploits the working class by extracting surplus value from its labour. In other words, workers produce a surplus as they work more than the socially necessary labour time. However, they work for the capitalists that appropriate this surplus. Thus, he addresses that the relations between capital and labour are intrinsically antagonistic.

In short, Marx develops a critical understanding of the dynamics of capitalism and the potentialities of class struggles toward political, social and economic transformations. What he adds to our understanding is that the fundamental categories of thinking are historical. His writings call our attention to uncovering our present-day world in order to challenge current Western thinking about free markets.

Box 7. A biographical note.

Karl Heinrich Marx was born in Trier, Germany, in 1818. Because of his interest in philosophy, he abandoned the law studies. In the summer of 1843, after marrying, Marx moved to Paris, where he focused his activities ion the studies of political economy and the French Revolution. After being expelled from France in 1845, he remained in Brussels until the outbreak of the February revolution. In 1848, after being expelled by the Belgian government, he returned to Paris. However, after a short period, he was forced to leave the country and then moved to London. There, in addition to his studies and writings, he got deeply involved with the workers' struggles and turned out to be a cofounder of the International Working Men's Association. Karl Marx died in London in 1883 [1].

Box 8. Selected works.

Books 1844. Economic and Philosophic Manuscripts of 1844 1845. The German Ideology 1847. Wage, Capital and Labour 1848. Manifesto of the Communist Party 1857. Grundrisse 1859. A Contribution to the Critique of Political Economy 1862. Theories of Surplus Value 1867. Capital, Volume I 1885. Capital, Volume II (posthumously published by Engels) 1894. Capital, Volume III (posthumously published by Engels)

2.1.2. Key Concepts

When reading Karl Marx, you must remember that:

1. The capitalist economic system is based on a mode of production for trade in the markets.
2. Workers are formally free persons. However, the subordination of labour to capital is the central feature of capitalism. Workers produce a surplus as they work more hours than those that are the socially necessary labour time.

Capitalists exploit the working class by extracting this surplus value. Capitalists appropriate this surplus.

3. The progressive movement of capital can be referred as "money generating money".
4. The real subsumption of labour refers to the subordination of workers, on a large scale, to machinery in the capitalist production. The alienating effects of the mechanization of labour overwhelms all social dynamics.

2.1.3. Reading Passages: A Contribution to the Critique of Political Economy

The Reading Passages presented below were written by Karl Marx and were published in the book *A Contribution to the Critique of Political Economy,* 1859 [2]. In order to have in-depth understanding of Marx's contribution, we elaborated a summary of the main ideas.

Reading Passages	***Summary of the Main Ideas***
Commodities now confront one another in a dual form, really as use-values and nominally as exchange-values. They represent now for one another the dual form of labour contained in them, since the particular concrete labour actually exists as their use-value, while universal abstract labour-time assumes an imaginary existence in their price, in which they are all alike embodiments of the same substance of value, differing only quantitatively.	*Each commodity is a use-value and an exchange-value measured in universal abstract labour-time.*
Since labour-time is the intrinsic measure of value, why use another extraneous standard as well? Why is exchange-value transformed into price? Why is the value of all commodities computed in terms of an exclusive commodity, which thus becomes the adequate expression of exchange-value, *i.e.*, money?(...) Commodities are the direct products of isolated independent individual kinds of labour, and through their alienation in the course of individual exchange they must prove that they are general social labour, in other words, on the basis of commodity production, labour becomes social labour only as a result of the universal alienation of individual kinds of labour.	*Social labour is on the basis of commodity production for exchange. A labour theory of value suggests that the standard that we can use to explain that the relative value of various commodities is the amount of labour required to produce them.*
The commodity-owners entered the sphere of circulation merely as guardians of commodities. Within this sphere they confront one another in the antithetical roles of buyer and seller, one personifying a sugar-loaf, the other gold. Just as the sugar-loaf becomes gold, so the seller becomes a buyer. These distinctive social characters are, therefore, by no means due to individual human nature as such, but to the exchange relations of persons who produce their goods in the specific form of commodities. So little does the relation of buyer and seller represent a purely individual relationship that they enter into it only in so far as their individual labour is negated, that is to say, turned into money as non-individual labour. It is therefore as absurd to regard buyer and seller, these bourgeois economic types, as eternal social forms of human individuality, as it is preposterous to weep over them as signifying the abolition of individuality.	*The analysis of commodities for exchange is important in understanding the historical and social nature of the capitalist exchange system.*

Contd.....

Reading Passages	*Summary of the Main Ideas*
The conclusion which follows from this is, not that production, distribution, exchange and consumption are identical, but that they are links of a single whole, different aspects of one unit.	*The economic system is an organic entity.*

2.1.4. Modern Concerns About the Concept of Capital

Many controversies have arisen from the concept of capital that highlighted broad economic, social and political challenges of the capitalist mode of production.

More recently, Thomas Piketty's book *Capital in the 20th century* has been globally analysed, mainly because of his empirical research, developed with other scholars [3]. His conclusions about the historical growth in wealth and income inequality took into account the past three centuries in high-income countries. Among the main findings, Piketty highlights:

- There has been a general trend towards greater economic inequality, mainly within generations;
- Deliberate policies, mainly progressive taxation that affected inherited wealth, between 1914 and 1945, help to explain the evolution of a high degree of economic equality within Europe in the period post World War II;
- After the 1970s, inherited wealth turned out to be re-introduced in many European countries. This trend of patrimonial capitalism had been relevant in the late 19th century;
- Between 1977 and 2007, 1% of the richest people in the United States appropriated almost 60% of the increase in the American national income. This fact has been mainly associated to the rise of the "supermanagers" in the corporative world.

David Harvey has been critical of Piketty's neoclassical definition of capital that related capital to the stock of all assets held by private individuals, corporations and governments that can be traded in the markets [4].

Proceeding from a Marxian background, Harvey addresses that Piketty's concept of capital as a stock of assets traded in the markets excludes the apprehension of capital as a social process of production where capitalists and workers are interrelated.

In the current global setting, social relations have been shaped to follow market flexibility. As a result, employment has become a key variable in business "rationalization". Indeed, while recent changes in the capitalist mode of production favoured increasing competitiveness and good corporate governance criteria, the social outcomes in terms of employment and working conditions have resulted in growing informality, less powerful trade unions, income and wealth concentration. As a matter of fact, global social and economic inequality reveals tensions between the growing power of concentrated financial power and the unattended social needs.

2.1.5. Further Reading

1. Anderson, P. (1976). *Considerations on Western Marxism*. London: New Left Books.
2. Bottomore, T. (Ed.) (1991). *Dictionary of Marxist Thought*. Oxford: Blackwell Publishers
3. Callari, A., Cullenberg, S., & Biewener, C. (Eds.) (1995). *Marxism in the Postmodern Age. Confronting the New World Order*. New York: Guilford Press.
4. Leopold, D. (2007). *The Young Karl Marx: German Philosophy, Modern Politics, and Human Flourishing.* Cambridge: Cambridge University Press.
5. McLellan, D. (2007). *Marxism after Marx*. New York: Palgrave Macmillan.
6. Ollman, B. (1977). *Alienation*: Marx's Conception of Man in a Capitalist Society. Cambridge: Cambridge University Press.
7. Sitton, J. F. (1996). *Modern Marxian Theory. Class Formation and Social Conflict in Contemporary Capitalism*. New York: State University of New York Press.

2.2. Michal Kalecki on Degree of Monopoly and Class Struggle

2.2.1. Setting the Scene

Michal Kalecki's theory of effective demand focuses on the relationship between spending, production, prices and functional income distribution. In the late 1930s, he published the book *The Determinants of Distribution of the National Income* where he presents a model where the variables capitalist consumption, investment and consumption of workers are related to the respective sector of integrated production: capitalist consumption goods, investment goods and consumption goods for workers. The value of the production of each economic sector corresponds to the value added that is equal to the sum of profits and wages in each sector.

According to Kalecki, some relevant factors affect the functional income distribution between profits and wages, such as the degree of monopoly, the weight of labour costs in direct costs and the composition of the industrial structure. Given the income distributive factors in each sector, the aggregate product and the aggregate profits are determined by the aggregate amount of investment and of capitalist consumption. The more capitalists spend on investment and consumption, the greater their profits. The aggregate amount of workers' consumption is conditioned by the levels of spending of capitalists in investment and consumption.

In his analysis of contemporary capitalism, Kalecki addresses that functional income distribution is connected with the main features of market structures where firms hold market power to fix their prices above direct costs (wages and raw materials). The role that the markup has on influencing prices and real wages introduces challenges related to class struggle not just between capitalists and workers but also between capitalists competing for market shares.

His research on contemporary market structures shows how the capitalist class fixes prices and strengthens its power relative to labour. In modern economies, prices could be: i) Based on demand, particularly for raw materials and commodity prices, since within an economic cycle changes can occur in the costs of raw materials during periods of high demand when prices are rising; ii) Based on costs, particularly for industrial products prices firms set prices adding a mark-up over direct costs.

In pricing strategies, the markup of a product is the addition of a profit margin to direct costs (raw materials, wages and resources). The profit margin of a product reflects the competitive features of the market and the cyclical dynamics of monopolistic capitalism. The addition of a profit margin reveals the degree of monopoly. In other words, this addition expresses the market power of a firm in an industry. It is related to the degree of conflict between capitalists and the relative power of capitalists and workers.

Kalecki suggests that the measure of the level of degree of monopoly refers to the ratio of prices to direct costs. A firm's ability to raise prices above direct costs results from its market power to affect the degree of monopoly in the industry. In other words, if firms face very limited competition, it is much freer to vary the prices of their products above direct costs than when they face substantial pressure from competitors.

Indeed, price flexibility or price rigidity is conditioned to firms' market power. The degree of monopoly can be affected by factors such as the influence of the process of concentration of the industry; promotions through product differentiation and advertising; changes in the relationship between overhead costs and direct costs.

In addition to these factors, the strength of trade unions can reduce the degree of monopolization in the markets. Throughout an expansionary period, trade unions could be active in defending higher nominal wages and thus they could put pressure on the evolution of markups. Adversely, during depressions, if unions accept nominal wage cuts, this could result in higher markups if prices remained constant because of the higher degree of monopoly of firms and industries.

Box 9. A biographical note.

Michal Kalecki was born in the city of Łódź, Poland, in the year of 1899. After abandoning his engineering studies in Warsaw, Kalecki returned in 1925 to his family city to help his parents. In addition to short-term teaching jobs, he wrote many journalistic articles. Because of his political interests, he read Tugan-Baranowski, Rosa Luxemburg and Karl Marx. In late 1929s, he started working at the Institute for the Study of Business Cycles and Prices in Warsaw as a consultant on cartels. After the 1930s, he received a Rockefeller Fellowship on behalf of the excellent reputation of his analysis on business cycles. Throughout the World War II, he developed research studies at the Oxford Institute of Statistics. Later on, he joined the International Labour Office in Montreal and, in 1946, he moved to New York in order to work at the United Nations Secretariat. In 1955, he returned to Poland and became an important economic advisor to government organizations, university professor and member of the Polish Academy of Sciences. After 1968, although he resigned all his posts and retired, Kalecki continued to develop research activities. In 1970, he was nominated for the Nobel Prize for Economics but died on 17 April 1970 in Warsaw [5].

Box 10. Selected works.

Articles 1942. A Theory of Profits 1943. Political Aspects of Full Employment 1962.Observations on the Theory of Growth 1970.Theories of Growth in Different Social Systems *Books* 1939. Essays in the Theory of Economic Fluctuations 1943. Studies in Economic Dynamics 1954. Theory of Economic Dynamics: An essay on cyclical and long-run changes in capitalist economy 1966. Studies in the Theory of Business Cycles, 1933–1939 1971. Selected Essays on the Dynamics of the Capitalist Economy, 1933–1970 *Collected writings* 1990. Collected Works of Michal Kalecki. Volume 1. Capitalism: Business Cycles and Full Employment 1991. Collected Works of Michal Kalecki. Volume 2. Capitalism: Economic Dynamics 1997. Collected Works of Michal Kalecki. Volume 3. Studies in Applied Economics

2.2.2. Key Concepts

When reading Michal Kalecki, you must remember that:

1. The Kaleckian theory of effective demand articulates the relations between decisions of spending, production and pricing along with their outcomes in

terms of aggregate income and income distribution. In this theoretical approach, the variables of final spending - capitalist consumption, investment and consumption of workers - are connected with economic sectors where firms produce final goods: capitalist consumption goods (D1), investment goods (D1) and consumption goods for workers (D3).

2. The economic matrix presents the global product of the capitalist economy. The economic matrix represents three economic sectors of vertically integrated production, which produce respectively: capital goods; consumer goods for capitalists; consumer goods for workers. At the same time, the economic matrix shows the income distribution between profits (P1, P2 and P3) and wages (W1, W2, W3) in each economic sector. The advantage of considering the production of final goods – the intermediate goods are produced by the departments that use them- is that the value of the production of each department corresponds to the value added, *i.e.*, the sum of profits and wages.
3. The factors affecting income distribution include: the degree of monopoly; the weight of labour costs in direct costs, and the composition of the industrial structure.
4. The evolution of prices depends on the firms' market power, which in turn is affected by industrial concentration. If firms face very limited competition, they are much freer to vary the prices of their products than if they face substantial pressure from competitors. Indeed, in market structures where firms hold market power, they fix their prices above direct costs (wages and raw materials).

2.2.3. Reading Passages: A Theory of Profits

The Reading Passages presented below were written by Michal Kalecki and were published in the article A *Theory of Profits,* 1942 [6]. In order to have in-depth understanding of Kalecki's contribution, we elaborated a summary of the main ideas.

Reading Passages	***Summary of the Main Ideas***
By gross profits we shall mean depreciation and net undistributed profits, dividends, interest, rent and also managerial salaries, all after payment of direct taxes. The receivers of this type of income we call capitalists. The rest of incomes are wages (also taken net of direct taxes) and doles.	*The main concern is the functional distribution of income between labour and capital.*
Now, it is clear that they may decide to consume and to invest more in a certain short period than in the preceding period, but they cannot decide to earn more.	*Capitalist consumption and investment are autonomous variables, that is to say, their levels are not restrained by past levels of income.*

Contd.....

Reading Passages	*Summary of the Main Ideas*
We may now conclude that the real gross profits in a given short period are determined by decisions of capitalists as to their consumption and investment formed in the past, subject to the correction for the unexpected changes in the volume of stocks.	*The decisions of capitalista can move the economic system towards higher levels of income and, therefore, determine higher amounts of gross profits.*
Since profits in a given short period are determined by capitalists' decisions as to their consumption and investment formed in the past, the factors determining the distribution of income will affect not real profits but the real wage bill, and consequently the national output.	*Changes in the factors of income distribution affect the evolution of real wages.*
If, for instance, the degree of monopoly increases, and, as a result, so does the ratio of profits to wages, real profits do not change, but the real wage bill falls, first because of the falling real wage rate, and secondly because of the consequent reduction in demand for wage goods, and thus of output and. employment in the wage-good industries.	*Changes in the factor of distribution called as degree of monopoly affect the evolution of real wages, and therefore, the demand for wage goods and the levels of output and employment in the wage-good industries.*

2.2.4. Modern Concerns About Income Distribution

The global finance-led accumulation regime has presented some distinctive features. A redefinition of the role of the state has justified privatization and deregulation in product, labour and financial markets. Changes in macroeconomic policies turned out to focus inflationary targets and financial stability instead of employment goals. Indeed, financial liberalization has also undermined the ability of national governments to expand budgets and promote economic planning in order to favour sustainable growth. Besides, there has been a redefinition of business models and working conditions [7].

Along with these new business strategies, new perspectives on social reproduction have been driven by short-term profits and competition. Mergers and acquisitions have fostered ownership changes, financial restructuring and company efficiency. Beyond the implementation of downsizing strategies, social struggles tend to increase as restructuring actions reshape as working conditions have been constantly reorganized and reshaped on behalf of financial commitments.

Changing labour organizing principles have coped with the dictates of increasing capital mobility, higher productivity and efficiency. In addition to changes in employment and working conditions, attacks on labour unions or the diminishing organizational strength of collective demands need to be underlined. In truth, the current features of labour markets have favoured the insecurity of workers, mainly young people, and precarious jobs.

As Kalecki warned, the patterns of growth and of functional income distribution are interconnected. In the current setting, the evolution of functional income distribution has shown a reduction of the workers′ share of aggregate income. At this respect, the Nobel laureate Joseph Stiglitz, in his book *The Price of Inequality,* points out some relevant issues to address in any attempt the rethink the foundations of current wealth and income inequality [8]. Stiglitz highlights that:

a. The increased value of existing assets helps to explain a large fraction of the increase in wealth.
b. Credit expansion has favoured increases in land and fixed asset prices that are part of rich people asset portfolios,
c. Higher market power of investors and managers and weaken workers' bargaining power reveal the deleterious consequences of abusive corporate power in terms of functional income distribution.

More recently, the current era of austerity – and its impacts on job creation and wages - is certainly affecting day-to-day life of workers and income distribution trends. Many governments now face hard decisions to deal with the impacts of the debt overhang: less spending on social policies, low growth, besides increasing social inequalities. Indeed, policy challenges include rising government debt and sovereign default risk. After adopting austerity programs, many governments have disappointed their citizens. As a result, there are social and political conflicts within the current crisis setting: the policy outcomes on livelihoods and the subordination of social needs to restricted public budgets on behalf of the bail-outs of the financial system and global investors' demands.

Indeed, systemic tensions will be deepened by austerity programs. Macroeconomic adjustments that privilege fiscal austerity and real wage flexibility can be costly, socially and politically.

2.2.5. Further Reading

1. King, J. E. (2003). *A History of Post Keynesian Economics since 1936.* Cheltenham: Edward Elgar.
2. Kreisler, P. (1997). Keynes, Kawecki and the General Theory. In G. C. Harcourt, P. A. Reach (Eds.). *A "Second Edition" of the General Theory.* London: Routledge.
3. López, J., & Assous, M. (2010). *Michal Kalecki*. Great Thinkers in Economics. New York: Palgrave Macmillan.
4. Toporowski, J. (2013). *Michal Kalecki: An Intellectual Biography*. Volume 1: *Rendezvous in Cambridge, 1899-1939*. New York: Palgrave Macmillan.
5. Mott, T. (2010). *Kalecki's Principle of Increasing Risk and Keynesian*

Economics. London: Routledge.
6. Sadowski, Z. L., & Szeworski, A. (2004). *Kalecki's Economics Today*. London: Routledge.
7. Sebastiani, M. (Ed.) (1989). *Kalecki's Relevance Today*. London: Macmillan.

2.3. John Galbraith on Modern Institutions

2.3.1. Setting the Scene

John Kenneth Galbraith's contribution to Economics privileges the changing economic reality and the role of institutions in modern capitalism. When describing the dual character of modern economies, Galbraith pays special attention to the system of large corporations that is characterized by the separation of ownership and control. He develops a new view on the strategies and policies of large corporations as their outcomes turn out to influence the whole economy.

His fundamental critique of neoclassical economic theory is related to the role of power in the analysis of markets. In the book *The New Industrial State* (1967), while describing his ideas on the modern capitalist corporation, Galbraith builds the foundations of his theoretical approach on economic power.

In the modern corporation, the technostructure is the group of experts – such as managers, economists, engineers, lobbyists - who increasingly make technical decisions by planning corporate growth. Among other actions, Galbraith highlights the process of corporate planning where the group of experts reveal all its power to influence the future of the large corporation.

Box 11. A biographical note.

John Kenneth Galbraith was born in Canada in the year of 1908 and became an American citizen in 1937. After graduating from the Ontario Agricultural College in 1931, he got a Ph.D in Agricultural Economics (1934) at the University of California.
After becoming a tutor at Harvard University, where he worked intermittently in the period between 1934 and 1939. In this period, he was influenced by the ideas of John Maynard Keynes during a fellowship at Cambridge University.
Later on, Galbraith taught at Princeton University from 1939 to 1940 and became professor of economics at Harvard in 1949. He also participated in the board of editors of Fortune magazine (1943-1948).
He served in the public service in the administrations of Franklin D. Roosevelt, Harry S. Truman, John F. Kennedy, and Lyndon B. Johnson. He was appointed as the American ambassador to India under President Kennedy.
Galbraith died aged 95, in 2006, in Cambridge, Massachussets [9].

Taking into account the business strategies and market features after the 1950s, mainly in the United States, Galbraith addresses the inner links between large corporations' growth and the expanded role for government in modern economies.

Box 12. Selected works.

Books
1938. Modern Competition and Business Policy
1952 A Theory of Price Control
1952. American Capitalism: The Concept of Countervailing Power
1958. The Affluent Society
1967. The New Industrial State
1973. Economics and the Public Purpose
1977. The Age of Uncertainty
1879. The Nature of Masa Poverty
1983. The Anatomy of Power
1997. The Good Society: The Humane Agenda.
2004. The Economics of Innocent Fraud

First, the large corporation seeks further growth by shaping consumer attitudes as a consequence of advertising and marketing strategies. Indeed, large corporations are sovereign in the markets of goods and services. Second, the large size of corporations results from economies of scale, research & development and investments in new technology. In this attempt, the role of public policies is outstanding. Third, the modern corporation seeks to guarantee the expansion of markets and profits through further government´s actions.

2.3.2. Key Concepts

When reading John Kenneth Galbraith, you must remember that:

1. The modern industrial system refers to the group of corporations that has control of a large part of the output produced in key sectors of the economy.
2. The technostructure controls the industrial shareholders and plan the long-term growth of the corporation. The technostructure does not act to maximize profits, but principally to maintain the organization in the market and to ensure its further expansion by using retained profits.
3. The corporations of the modern "industrial system" develop informal practices of pricing in conjunction with strategies of marketing, advertisement, research & development, among others, to favour the feasibility of long-term planning.
4. There is a set of deep interconnections between large corporations and nation-states.

2.3.3. Reading Passages: The New Industrial State

The Reading Passages presented below were written by John Galbraith and were published in the book The *New Industrial State,* 1967 [10]. In order to have in-depth understanding of Galbraith's contribution, we elaborated a summary of the main ideas.

Reading Passages	*Summary of the Main Ideas*
The innovations and alterations in economic life in this century, and more especially since the beginning of World War II, have, by any calculation, been great. The most visible has been the application of increasingly intricate and sophisticated technology to the production of things.	*After World War II, the role of technology has been outstanding in industrial production.*
Eighty years ago the corporation was the instrument of its owners and a projection of their personalities. The names of these principals—Carnegie, Rockefeller, Harriman, Mellon, Guggenheim, Ford—were known across the land. They are still known, but for the art galleries and philanthropic foundations they established and their descendants who are in politics. The men who now head the great corporations are unknown.	*In modern corporations, there has been a separation between ownership and control in business firms. Large corporations are owned by millions of shareholders who hire professional managers to run the company.*
There has been a further massive growth in the apparatus of persuasion and exhortation that is associated with the sale of goods. In its cost and in the talent it commands, this activity is coming increasingly to rival the effort devoted to the production of goods. Measurement of the exposure, and susceptibility, of human beings to this persuasion is itself a flourishing science.	*The role of marketing has increased in order to shape consumers' behaviour. The power of large corporations has been noticed in the creation of new consumers' demands.*
When investment in technological development is very high, a wrong technical judgment or a failure in persuading consumers to buy the product can be extremely expensive. The cost and associated risk can be greatly reduced if the state pays for more exalted technical development or guarantees a market for the technically advanced product. Suitable justification— national defense, national prestige, deeply felt public need, as for alternatives to petroleum products—can readily be found. Exemption from the damaging charge that the action is socialist is automatically forthcoming. Modern technology thus defines a growing function of the modern state.	*There is a growing interaction between the advance of technology and the support of the state to the viability of private investments.*
The two parts of the economy—the world of the technically dynamic, massively capitalized and highly organized corporations on the one hand and of the hundreds of thousands of small and traditional proprietors on the other—are very different. It is not a difference of degree but a difference which invades every aspect of economic organization and behavior, including the motivation to effort itself. It will be convenient, even in advance of more formulation, to have a name for the part of the economy which is characterized by the large corporations. One is readily at hand; I shall refer to it as the Planning System. The planning system, in turn, is the dominant feature of the New Industrial State.	*The economic organization and dynamics are characterized by a duality because of the asymmetries that can be noted between large and small businesses. The role of large corporations is decisive and it depends on a planning system that is the main feature of the New Industrial State.*

2.3.4. Modern Concerns About Business Strategies

More recently, changes in corporate power and governance strategies overwhelmed the advance of financial globalization. Indeed, the process of financialization has radically changed the strategies and practices of banks, non-banks and non-financial institutions. Among the changes in their balance sheets:

- Families have increased the levels of indebtedness;
- Firms have diversified assets in their portfolios;.
- The shadow banking has increased its role in the economy and turned out to control the amount and direction of huge investment flows [11].

Indeed, research evidences from corporations and management practices, in the U.S. and Europe, described that business strategies till the 1970s privileged decisions called as 'retain and reinvest', that is to say, decisions to retain profits into the company and reinvest them into productive capacity [12]. However, business strategies have changed after the 1970s. In the context of financialization, changes in business practices have been stimulated by new priorities towards creating increasing shareholder value [13].

In this setting, mergers and acquisitions, higher productivity and global competition have promoted short-term profits [14]. As a result, not only operational strategies in production (suppliers, labour, *etc.*) but also marketing and commercialization strategies (logistics, mark-up, market share, customer relationship, *etc.* have been relevant to face productivity challenges and efficiency targets.

As Galbraith highlighted, corporate strategies and power relations are intertwined. Beyond current short-term business performance targets there has been implemented a deep capitalist reorganization of employment and working conditions that enhanced increasing inequality and loss of rights.

2.3.5. Further Reading

1. Hession, C. (1972). *John Kenneth Galbraith and His Critics*. New York: New American Library.
2. Keaney, M. (2001). *Economist with a Public Purpose: Essays in Honour of John Kenneth Galbraith*. London: Routledge.
3. Parker, R. (2005). *John Kenneth Galbraith: His Life, His Politics, His Economics*. New York: Farrar, Straus, and Giroux.
4. Reisman, D. A. (1980). *Galbraith and Market Capitalism*. New York: New York University Press.
5. Sobel, R. (1980). *The Worldly Economists*. New York: Free Press.
6. Stanfield, J.R., & Stanfield, J. B.(2004). *Interviews with John Kenneth Galbraith*. Jackson: University Press of Mississippi.
7. Stone, I. (1970). *There Was Light: Autobiography of a University: Berkeley, 1868–1968*. Garden City, N.Y.: Doubleday.
8. Waligorski, C. (2006). *John Kenneth Galbraith: The Economist as Political Theorist*. Lanham, Md: Rowman & Littlefield.

2.4. Policy Tools: Re-balancing Corporate Power

Changes in corporate power and governance strategies have created new business models after the 1970s. In this setting, private equity funds have increased their role as employers in the global setting. In this scenario, corporate decisions and working conditions have been increasingly subordinated to speculative financial commitments. Managers and owners of firms have privileged short-term financial performance and shareholder value. As a result, the participation of total wages has diminished in aggregate income.

Considering this background, the promotion of a regulatory task force in business to achieve sustainable and inclusive growth should include corporate governance policies [15]. Corporate governance regulation should discourage the search for short-term profits and should emphasize the following topics:

- Higher transparency in public reporting;
- Changes in supervision methods and oversight of corporate governance by regulatory authorities;
- New approaches to taxation of capital gains that result from the sale of assets in the context of mergers and acquisitions;
- New enforcement approaches to relevant employer obligations by private equity funds.

Further measures oriented to increase transparency in public reporting requirements should consider:

- **Financial strategies.** Reports should include information about: i) total amounts of debt; ii) features of debt contracts: types, maturities, rates (floating or fixed), payment schedules and flows of debt service; iii) fees paid in mergers and acquisitions;
- **Business plans.** Reports should include information about: i) strategies to close plants and exit; ii) strategies to manage cash reserves, financial assets and intangible assets; iii) sale and possible lease-back of real estate; iv) strategies to manage sources of funds for investments, training, and research& development; v) strategies to change working conditions.

In addition, public policies oriented to tax regulation should include i) tax deductibility of the flows of debt service, ii) tax on capital gains and tax havens. Indeed, it is time to favour tax systems that could banish short-term returns that result from the financial management of corporations.

REFERENCES

[1] Engels F. Karl Marx 1869. Retrieved from: https://www.marxists.org/archive/marx/bio/marx/eng-

1869.htm

[2] Marx K. A Contribution to the Critique of Political Economy 1859. Retrieved from: https://www.marxists.org/archive/marx/works/download/Marx_Contribution_to_the_Critique_of_Political_Economy.pdf

[3] Piketty T. Capital in the Twenty-First Century. Cambridge, MA: Belknap Press 2014. [http://dx.doi.org/10.4159/9780674369542]

[4] Madi M A C. Piketty and Harvey: on the Concept of Capital and Economics Education 2014. Retrieved from: https://weapedagogy.wordpress.com/2014/06/09/piketty-and-harvey-on-the-co-cept-of-capital-and-economics-education/

[5] Toporowski J. 2013. *Michal Kalecki: An Intellectual Biography. Volume 1: Rendezvous in Cambridge, 1899-1939.* New York: Palgrave Macmillan. Figura, I. (2005). Profiles of World Economists: Michal Kalecki. *Biatec,* XIII, 21–25. Retrieved from: http://www.nbs.sk/_img/Documents/BIATEC/BIA10_05/21_25.pdf

[6] Kalecki M. A Theory of Profits 1942. Retrieved from: https://esepuba.files.wordpress.com/2011/10/kalecki-1942.pdf [http://dx.doi.org/10.2307/2225784]

[7] Fligstein N. The architecture of markets Princeton, NJ: Princeton University Press Kumar, K (2005) From post-industrial to post-modern society. UK: Blackwell Publishing 2001.

[8] Stiglitz J. The Price of Inequality: How Today's Divided Society Endangers Our Future. New York: W. W. Norton & Company 2012.

[9] Editors of the New World Encyclopedia. John Kenneth Galbraith. 2017. New World Encyclopedia. Retrieved from: http://www.newworldencyclopedia.org/entry/John_Kenneth_Galbraith

[10] Galbraith JK. The New Industrial State. Princeton, NJ: Princeton University Press 2007.

[11] Seccareccia M. Financialization and the transformation of commercial banking; understanding the recent Canadian experience before and during the international financial crisis. J Post Keynes Econ 2012; 35(2): 277-300. [http://dx.doi.org/10.2753/PKE0160-3477350206]

[12] Lazonick W, O'Sullivan M. Maximizing shareholder value: a new ideology for corporate governance 2000. [http://dx.doi.org/10.1080/030851400360541]

[13] Froud J, Haslam C, Johal S, Williams K. Restructuring for shareholder value and its implications for labour 2000. [http://dx.doi.org/10.1093/cje/24.6.771]

[14] Madi MA. Old and new business models 2016. Retrieved from: https://weapedagogy.wordpress.com/2016/12/12/old-and-new-business-models/

[15] Madi MA. Mergers, downsizing and labour relations: rebalancing global business power. 2014.

CHAPTER 3

Money

Abstract: This chapter aims to present different perspectives on the theory of money. Firstly, we refer to Eugen von Böhm-Bawerk's theoretical approach developed in the late 1880s that highlights the concept of interest rate in the context of inter-temporal allocation decisions. Then, we consider John Maynard Keynes's contribution privileges that money is non-neutral and that the rate of interest is a monetary phenomenon. Finally, we include the Keynesian approach developed by James Tobin to monetary issues in bank money and banking strategies in order to clarify the dynamics of banks' decisions toward profitable assets.

Keywords: Interest rate, Non-neutrality of money, Process of bank money creation.

3. INTRODUCTION

Controversies about the role of money, interest rates and the banking system have been present in economic debates since the 18th century. Today, monetary issues continue to play an outstanding role in policy making. This chapter aims to present different perspectives on the theory of money.

First, we begin presenting the theoretical approach that Eugene von Böhm-Bawerk developed in the late 1880s. He was a relevant economist in the Austrian school of economic thought and turned out to highlight the concept of interest rate in the context of inter-temporal allocation decisions. In this approach, the value theory and the theory of capital are developed within a general equilibrium model.

Second, we highlight John Maynard Keynes's contribution to monetary theory that distances itself from Bohm Bawerk. In the 1930s, Keynes considered the particular features of the capitalist system as a monetary economy. In the 1930s, he highlighted the instability of the levels of spending, income and employment in the capitalist economic systems.

Finally, we considered the approach developed by James Tobin to monetary issues in bank money and banking strategies. Proceeding from the Keynesian background, in the 1950s, Tobin clarifies the dynamics of banks' decisions toward

Maria Alejandra Madi

profitable assets in order to show that banks create deposits in the process of lending and hold reserves after evaluating opportunity costs.

3.1. Eugen Von Böhm-Bawerk on Inter-Temporal Allocation

3.1.1. Setting the Scene

Eugen von Böhm-Bawerk extended the value theory to the analysis of inter-temporal allocation decisions. Indeed, the theory of value and the theory of interest developed within a general equilibrium model where the element of time is decisive to understand the inter-temporal decisions. Under this approach, the nominal interest rate, as the price of an exchange transaction, results from subjective valuations of buyers and sellers regarding present and future goods.

In the theoretical framework presented in 1889 in *The Positive Theory of Capital*, Böhm-Bawerk inquires how time influences the value of goods. Based on empirical evidence, he highlights that, considering the same quantity of goods of the same quality, the value of these present goods is higher than the value of future goods. The payment of interest directly reflects the inter-temporal value differential between present and future goods. Indeed, future goods are traded at a discount, or, in other words, present goods are being traded at a premium. This idea was an extension of Carl Menger´s subjective value theory to an inter-temporal calculus.

Böhm-Bawerk presents three causes for the lower valuation of future goods. Firstly, there is a discrepancy between the inter-temporal structures of the wants to be satisfied by consumption goods and the availability of those goods. Secondly, he includes the impatient of individuals. Thirdly, he presents the degree of roundaboutness of production that considers the average time distance between the labour inputs and the consumption good output produced by these labour inputs. The greater roundaboutness of production and therefore a greater labour productivity, in the supply of consumption goods for the future is allowed by the earlier availability of inputs. On behalf of the action of these three factors, Böhm-Bawerk concludes that the real interest rate is positive in a stationary general equilibrium.

In short, the level of interest rate depends, on the supply side, on time preferences and, on the demand side, on productiveness. At that period, great economists - such as Knut Wicksell, Irving Fisher, John Bates Clark, Gustav Cassel and Carl Menger - did accept his monetary theory fully. Later on, some economists of the Austrian school, in particular Hayek and Mises, built their contributions taking into account the contributions of Böhm-Bawerk´s to the theory of capital.

Box 13. A biographical note.

Eugen von Böhm-Bawerk was born in Austria in 1851. After finishing his doctorate in Law (1875) at the University of Vienna, he began a parallel progression from Law to Economics. In the early 1870s, Böhm-Bawerk worked at the Austrian ministry of finance for a short period.
His teaching career began in 1880 as a private lecturer of political economy at the University of Vienna. Between 1881 and 1889, he worked at the University of Innsbruck where got a steady position as professor in 1884.
Later on, he worked on the project of the reform of the Austrian tax code and proposed a modern version of an income tax. He was also ambassador to the German court (1897) and promoted to the House of Peers (1889).
In the period between 1895 and 1904, Böhm-Bawerk served as minister of finance. He aimed the strict adherence to the nation's gold standard and budget balance. After resigning, he returned to the University of Vienna and he was nominated vice-president (1907) and president (1911) of the Academy of Science.
Böhm-Bawerk died in the ear of 1914, in Kramsach, Austria [1].

Box 14. Selected works.

Books
1884. Capital and Interest
1889. The Positive Theory of Capita
1896. Karl Marx and the Close of his System

3.1.2. Key Concepts

When reading Eugene von Böhm-Bawerk, you must remember that:

1. The concept of utility is a pillar of the theory of value since the marginal utility of any good determines its value.
2. According to the subjective theory of value, the marginal utility refers to the amount of the utility that an individual gets with the consumption of additional units of a good.
3. The value of a good is dependent on the interaction between *want* and *provision*. The price or exchange value of a good results from the interaction of competitive forces of supply and demand.
4. The payment of interest directly reflects the inter-temporal value differential between present and future goods.

3.1.3. Reading Passages: The Rate of Interest

The Reading Passages presented below were written by Eugen von Böhm-Bawerk's and were published in the book *The positive theory of capital*, Book VI, Chapter 1, 1889 [2]. In order to have in-depth understanding of Böhm-Bawerk's contribution, we elaborated a summary of the main ideas.

Reading Passages	*Summary of the Main Ideas*
(…) the natural difference that exists between the value of present and the value of future goods. I have now to show that this difference of value is the source and origin of all Interest on Capital.	*The element of time is crucial to the understanding of all interest on capital. The payment of interest has a definite connection with the time when payment is made.*
A loan is nothing else than a real and true exchange of present goods for future goods; indeed, it is the simplest conceivable phenomenal form, and, to some extent, the ideal and type of such an exchange. The "lender," A, gives to the "borrower," B, a sum of present goods— say, present pounds sterling. B gets full and free possession of the goods to deal with as he likes, and, as equivalent, he gives into A's full and free possession a sum of entirely similar, but future, goods—say, next year's pounds sterling.	*The simplest case of the difference between present and future value of goods good is presented in a loan for consumption. In this case, there is a real and true exchange of a smaller amount of present money, or present goods, for a larger amount of future money or goods.*
(…) the prospect of interest induces saving and accumulation of capital, and thus, by making possible the adoption of more fruitful methods of production, becomes the cause of a more abundant provision for the whole people.	*The prospect of the difference between the present and the future value of goods induces higher saving, and therefore, higher investments in fixed capital.*
In this connection, the much-used and much-abused expression, "Reward of Abstinence," is in its proper place. The existence of interest cannot be theoretically explained by it: one cannot hope in using it to say anything about the essential nature of interest: everyone knows how much interest is simply pocketed without any "abstinence "that deserves reward.	*The proper existence of interest cannot be theoretically explained by the idea that the interest rate is a reward of abstinence.*
But, just as interest sometimes has its injurious accompaniments, so in its train it brings others, fortunately, that are beneficent and useful; and to these it is due that interest, which has its origin in quite different causes, acts, among other things, as a wage and as an inducement to save.	*The role of interest of capital is useful to the economy as it can be considered an incentive to save and a remuneration of the employer as a workman.*
I know very well that private saving is not the only possible way to the accumulation of capital, and that, even in the Socialist state, capital may be accumulated and added to. But the fact remains that private accumulation of capital is a proved fact, while socialist accumulation is not; —and there are, besides, some very serious a priori doubts whether it can be.	*In the capitalist system, private saving is required for capital accumulation and economic growth.*

3.1.4. Modern Concerns About the Level of Interest Rates

New political alignments allowed the process of global financial deregulation after the 1970s. As a result, the political power of financial overwhelmed the economic agenda policy where price stability and fiscal balance turned out to be the primary objectives of the economic policy. Prior to the 2007-2008 global crisis, inflation in many countries around the world remained at low levels and close to central banks' inflation target rates. However, credit and asset bubbles turned out to threaten the global macroeconomic stability.

Many of the debates about the roots of the 2007-2008 global crisis has privileged the failures of financial regulation and the role of Central Banks. Indeed, after the Global Crisis, academic economists and policy makers have actively participated in the debate about American and European monetary policies.

In the outcomes of the crisis, Central Banks have dealt with a triple challenge:

- how to contain the crisis
- how to prevent a recessionary downturn
- how to avoid enhancing financial instability in the form of inflationary pressures or asset and credit bubbles.

The Federal Reserve (FED) and the European Central Bank (ECB) have faced major global financial challenges together. After the bail-outs, their main concern has been whether there is a lower bound around zero percent on nominal interest rates. After the crisis, Central Banks managed the drop in aggregate spending by adopting quantitative easing policies. They also adjusted the policy interest rates to very low levels, almost close to zero [3].

Indeed, those central banks have focused on lender-of-last-resort program extensions. The main question is: to what extent central banks can deal with huge levels of leverage, structural flaws of financial innovations (securitization, structured finance, and derivatives above all) and lack of transparency in terms of risk management?

Central banks have shown that they can innovate and coordinate with other central banks on short notice when unprecedented situations of financial crisis arise. However, central banks cannot prevent financial crisis. Considering the menace of deepening the recession, the outcome of the central banks' management of nominal interest rates is that real interest rates may be (and may continue to be) negative. Despite the evolution of nominal and real interests, big banks have restricted new lending operations because of credit and market risks. Indeed, big banks have enlarged the amount of cash in order to cope with their own losses more easily in the future.

John Maynard Keynes rejected the theoretical approach of Böhm-Bawerk to interest rates. In the 1930s, Keynes addressed that the determinants of the interest rate are not related to inter-temporal allocation between consumption and saving, but to liquidity preference in a context of uncertainly in a monetary economy. In particular, Keynes explained that the liquidity trap was a period in which cash and bonds became perfect substitutes after policy interest rates have fallen to a very low level. In this setting, liquidity preference may be almost absolute.

In other words, central banks have difficulty in reducing interest rates at levels around or below zero since most people would demand money (cash) instead of holding assets which yields. In this setting, expansionary monetary policy, as Keynes warned, is not effective to influence aggregate spending.

The modern Keynesian literature addresses that monetary policy works effectively through expectations at zero bound levels. As a result, Central Bank's decision and practices are always relevant to the management of the investors' expectations about the level of future nominal and real interest rates.

Therefore, the question is how very low interest rates could translate into higher levels of aggregate spending. It is worth remembering that Central Banks consider that the monetary stimulus could foster economic growth in the short-run through different transmission channels:

- Credit expansion
- Increasing asset prices
- Demand for riskier assets
- Devaluated exchange rates

Up to now, the positive effects of these transmission channels on economic growth and employment have been far from certain. However, potential serious consequences for central banks could emerge. Actually, there is a threat that monetary policy could become subordinated to manage public debt burdens and to achieve financial stability.

3.1.5. Further Reading

1. Faber, M. (1979). *Introduction to Modern Austrian Capital Theory*. Berlin: Springer.
2. Hennings, K. (1997). *The Austrian Theory of Value and Capital: Studies in the Life and Work of Eugen von Böhm-Bawer*k. Cheltenham, UK: Edward Elgar:
3. Hilferding, R. (1904). Böhm-Bawerk's Criticism of Marx. In P. Sweezy (Ed.) (1949). *Karl Marx and the Close of his System by Eugen von Böhm-Bawerk and Böhm-Bawerk's Criticism of Marx by Rudolf Hilferding*. New York: Kelley.
4. Hennings, K. H. (1997). The Austrian Theory of Value and Capital: Studies in the Life and Works of Eugen Von Bohm-Bawerk. UK: Edward Elgar.
5. Kuenne, R.E. (1971). *Eugen von Böhm-Bawerk*. New York and London: Columbia University Press.
6. Schumpeter, J.A. (1952). *Ten Great Economists: From Marx to Keyne*s,

London: Allen & Unwin.
7. Stigler, G.J. (1941). *Production and Distribution Theories*. New York: Macmillan.

3.2. Keynes on the Non–Neutrality of Money

3.2.1. Setting the Scene

In the mid 1930s, John Maynard Keynes's contribution on monetary theory was the turning point in the understanding of the persistent unemployment observed in capitalist economies. In his view, the nature of the capitalism as a monetary economy explains a deep social problem: involuntary unemployment. In other words, Keynes highlighted the economic situation when people would want to find a job but businessmen are not hiring workers.

Keynes's theoretical approach rejected the classical economic theory that supposed the existence of self-regulating markets in capitalism. In accordance to the foundations of laissez-faire, free markets would automatically provide full employment. His criticism was oriented to the Say's law of the markets which highlighted that "supply creates its own demand" in a context where money is neutral. The idea of Say's law is that people's monetary income is consumed or saved. More saving will reduce the level of interest rates and this fact will induce investments in additional machines. Thus, through the mechanism of flexible interest rates, any decrease in consumption will be compensated by an increase in investment and the economy will maintain the equilibrium at full employment. Indeed, classical economists emphasized that the price system efficiently guides the adjustments of supply and demand in all markets towards full employment [4].

Indeed, the Law of Markets holds that that full employment could mainly be constrained by the lack of flexibility of nominal wages in the labour market on behalf of rigidities and/or restrictions imposed by employers, trade unions or governments. These rigidities and/or restrictions not only include labour regulation aimed to job protection, but also other institutional arrangements that could affect sectoral wage bargaining, labour market segmentation and discrimination. In short, in the classical framework, frictions were declared the main cause of unemployment. Frictional unemployment was studied by Arthur Pigou in *The Theory of Unemployment* (1933) [5]. According to Pigou, frictional unemployment is the kind of unemployment that arises from labour turnover and from people entering and leaving the labour force.

Keynes focuses on the analysis of instability of aggregate demand. His explanation addresses that the capitalist economy is not self-regulated – by contrast to the classical economists. In the famous book *The General Theory of*

Employment, Interest and Money (1936), his contribution to the understanding of the real-world economics privileges that money is non-neutral, that is to say, can affect the levels of spending, output and employment.

What Keynes adds to our understanding about real-world economics is that capitalist economies show levels of income below the full employment, *i.e.* productive potential. This is associated with the role that money plays. Money is the ultimate purpose of an entrepreneurial economy. Money is a store of value, that is to say, an asset. This is crucial for the apprehension of the roots of employment.

In *The General Theory*, he assesses that the primary driver of economic expansion should be located in the demand side. The theory of effective demand is crucial to explore the causes of unemployment and the determination of income in an entrepreneurial economy. He argues that employers decide about the amount of labour that they would hire based on expected profits.

In order to explain involuntary unemployment, Keynes highlights the role of uncertainty and expectations in wealth management. Indeed, businessmen decide about the level of employment in a monetary economy where the future about profits is uncertain. Businessmen could postpone decisions about production and investment and look for alternative assets for expanding their wealth.

Keynes believes that investment decisions are based on conventions. In any specific conjuncture, the average opinion of entrepreneurs about future profits refers to a conventional behaviour that is founded on precarious expectations about the future performance of aggregate spending. The expected return on investment - marginal efficiency of capital- is influenced by the degree of confidence of businessmen on this conventional behaviour.

According to Keynes, money, as the institution that founds the exchange system, links the present and the future. On behalf of his concern about the distributive consequences of the non-neutrality of money, Keynes deepened his understanding of the evolution of business models in the context of organized capital markets. In the old business model, businessmen were committed towards long-term investments, that is to say, the decisions about current investment were irrevocable in the future. However, in the new business model, investments are not irrevocable for them in the future since "liquidity" is favoured by organized capital markets. Indeed, the investor's new target is liquidity.

Keynes's contributions to economic policy highlights that governments should make interventions to reduce the level of involuntary unemployment. Through public anti-cyclical expenditure policies, for example, governments could dampen the effects of private investment instability on economic growth and on employment levels.

Box 15. A biographical note.

John Maynard Keynes was born in the city of Cambridge, England, in 1883. His father was an economist and he gave lectures in Moral Sciences at the University of Cambridge.
In 1902, Keynes started his studies at King's College where he earned a scholarship and received a bachelor in mathematics. While studying in Cambridge, he was influenced by the English philosopher George Moore's analytic tradition. After 1907, Keynes became a member of the "Bloomsbury Group" that was associated to English intellectuals.
After working as a clerk in the India Office, Keynes started his studies and work on probability. In the year of 1909, he became lecturer in Cambridge in the economics course that was founded by Alfred Marshall. Two years later, Keynes became editor of the *Economic Journal* and published his first book *Indian Currency and Finance* in 1913.
During the Great Depression, Keynes's ideas on counter-cyclical public spending got great support. At that time, he participated at the group called the "Cambridge Circus" that included Joan Robinson and Richard Kahn.
Between 1911 and 1945, Keynes turned out to be deeply involved in political affairs as: advisor to the Treasury, British Ministry of Financial Affair, representative of the Treasury at the Versailles Peace Conference, member of the directorate of the Bank of England, member of the House of Lords and British delegate at the Bretton Woods Conference. In addition to a successful career as a financial consultant and stock market investor, he also became curator of the National Gallery and administered the finance of Sadler's Well Ballet – later the Royal Ballet. Besides, he was head of the British Arts Council and o the founders of the Cambridge Arts Theatre.
After a heart attack and severe illness, Keynes died in 1946 [6].

Box 16. Selected works.

Articles
*1*937. The general theory of unemployment
1940. How to pay for the war
Books
1912. Indian Currency and Finance
1921. A Treatise on Probability
1923. A Tract on Monetary Reform
1930. A Treatise on Money
1936. The General Theory of Employment, Interest and Money
Collected writings
1973. The General Theory and After, Part I Preparation, vol. XIII of The Collected Writings of John Maynard Keynes
1973. The General Theory and After, Part II Defence and Development, vol. XIV of The Collected Writings of John Maynard Keynes

3.2.2. Key Concepts

When reading John Maynard Keynes, you must remember that:

1. In a monetary economy of production, money is the asset that has the highest degree of liquidity. In this economy, the higher degree of liquidity of a non-monetary asset depends on the possibility of converting this asset into cash at lower transaction costs in a particular period of time.
2. On behalf of the uncertain future and the alternatives of wealth accumulation, investment is the most volatile component of gross domestic output. Aggregate investment is an autonomous form of spending and its level is mainly conditioned by expected profits, the level of interest rates and business conventions. Total (or gross) investment spending is composed of: i) spending on capital goods, also called fixed capital, such as the purchase of plant and equipment either to replace existing capacity that is depreciating or to increase capacity; ii) inventories that firms hold to satisfy miscalculated demand on the final goods they produce.
3. Consumption and investment are linked through the flows of income. Changes in the level of investment spending provoke changes in income and consumption flows. The overall impact on the level of aggregate consumption depends on the marginal propensity to consume.
4. Considering the instability of income in the capitalist system and the structural presence of involuntary unemployment, Keynes highlights the role of anti-cyclical government interventions to manage aggregate demand by monetary and fiscal policies.

3.2.3. Reading Passages: The General Theory

The Reading Passages presented below were written by John Maynard Keynes and were published in the book *The General Theory of Employment, Interest, and Money,* Chapter 12, 1936 [7]. In order to have in-depth understanding of Keynes's contribution, we elaborated a summary of the main ideas.

Reading Passages	***Summary of the Main Ideas***
Decisions to invest in private business of the old-fashioned type were, however, decisions largely irrevocable, not only for the community as a whole, but also for the individual. With the separation between ownership and management which prevails today and with the development of organized investment markets, a new factor of great importance has entered in, which sometimes facilitates investment but sometimes adds greatly to the instability of the system.	*In the old business model, there was an irrevocable commitment towards investment. However, in the new business model, the decisions about what amount and where to invest are no more an irrevocable commitment for investors and managers. Indeed, investment is not irrevocable since liquidity is the target.*

Contd.....

Reading Passages	*Summary of the Main Ideas*
(...).the daily revaluations of the Stock Exchange, though they are primarily made to facilitate transfers of old investments between one individual and another, inevitably exert a decisive influence on the rate of current investment. For there is no sense in building up a new enterprise at a cost greater than that at which a similar existing enterprise can be purchased; whilst there is an inducement to spend on a new project what may seem an extravagant sum, if it can be floated off on the Stock Exchange at an immediate profit. Thus certain classes of investment are governed by the average expectation of those who deal on the Stock Exchange as revealed in the price of shares, rather than by the genuine expectations of the professional entrepreneur.	*Short-term speculation became the order of the day while the Stock Exchange turned out to be a benchmark to future investments. The daily revaluations of the Stock Exchange have a decisive influence on the rate of current investment.*
Thus the professional investor is forced to concern himself with the anticipation of impending changes, in the news or in the atmosphere, of the kind by which experience shows that the mass psychology of the market is most influenced. This is the inevitable result of investment markets organized with a view to so-called 'liquidity'. Of the maxims of orthodox finance none, surely, is more anti-social than the fetish of liquidity, the doctrine that it is a positive virtue on the part of investment institutions to concentrate their resources upon the holding of 'liquid' securities. It forgets that there is no such thing as liquidity of investment for the community as a whole.	*The dominance of short-term speculation instead of long-term investment has major economic and social implications. Increasing speculation in financial markets and the search for liquidity are incompatible with society claims of employment and growth.*
If I may be allowed to appropriate the term speculation for the activity of forecasting the psychology of the market, and the term enterprise for the activity of forecasting the prospective yield of assets over their whole life, it is by no means always the case that speculation predominates over enterprise. As the organisation of investment markets improves, the risk of the predominance of speculation does, however, increase.	*The risk of speculation reveals the non-neutrality of money in the capitalist system. The new business model has increased the potential conflicts between short- run and long-run decisions as speculative expectations of investors must be accomplished.*
Speculators may do no harm as bubbles on a steady stream of enterprise. But the position is serious when enterprise becomes the bubble on a whirlpool of speculation. When the capital development of a country becomes a by-product of the activities of a casino, the job is likely to be ill-done. The measure of success attained by Wall Street, regarded as an institution of which the proper social purpose is to direct new investment into the most profitable channels in terms of future yield, cannot be claimed as one of the outstanding triumphs of laissez-faire capitalism which is not surprising, if I am right in thinking that the best brains of Wall Street have been in fact directed towards a different object.	*Financial speculation negatively influences the evolution of the levels of investment, product and employment.*

3.2.4. Modern Concerns About Finance, New Business Models and Labour

Throughout the last decades, the emphasis on short-term performance and the increasing power of global investors provoked deep impacts on business strategies led by private equity funds. For example, in the private equity business model, managers are designated to monitor the private equity funds' portfolio companies on their behalf. Private equity funds belong to the current complex landscape of institutional investors. Indeed, institutional investors could be classified as i) traditional investors– such as insurance companies, pension and investment funds; ii) alternative investors – such as private equity, hedge and sovereign wealth funds [8].

Private equity investments must be examined in the context of financialization that favours the power of global centralized capital to shape global investment flows could threaten the stability of a modern economy of production.

Indeed, private equity firms are considered a new financial phenomenon that uses a combination of equity and debt to access pension funds, sovereign wealth funds and insurance companies, for instance, to invest in targeted companies that are not traded publicly. The investment in a targeted company (investment buyout) depends on short-run expectations about profits, anticipated dividends and fees - before selling the company. Indeed, although these funds hold illiquid assets (companies), the exit strategies reveal the search for liquidity that influence the length of maturity of the investments.

Within the private equity business model, this speculative trend threatens the evolution of investment trends and the way business are run. In truth, private investment is responsible for an increasing number of mergers and acquisitions—a process that can be extremely disruptive to employees. Thus, the advance of the private equity business model has increased the potential conflicts between short and long-run decisions as the financial targets of investors must be rapidly accomplished. As a result, the growing of the so called "liquidity" is incompatible with society claims of employment and income equality

Job creation, working conditions, social rights and benefits have been decisively affected by private equity debt management and exit strategies. Under the euphemisms of downsizing, the extraction of short-run cash-flows fosters cost reductions after the takeovers and threatens investments in operations and product development. Exit strategies add more pressures on activist operational practices during the holding period, such as:

- Substitution of expensive workforce with robots;
- Further cost reduction through closures, outsourcing and crowdsourcing;
- Lower spending on research & development;
- Reduction of workers' rights, benefits and pension plans [9].

Indeed, the required labour flexibility has deep effects on employment and working conditions, outsourcing jobs and workers' rights. As the philosopher and sociologist Zygmunt Bauman warned in his book *Liquid Modernity,* labour market flexibility enhances the spread of short-term labour contracts, rolling labour contracts or even no labour contracts at all [10].

As Keynes warned, the business environment is particularly influenced by finance. Indeed, finance turned out to be in itself an important driver of transformations in employment trends and social benefits. One of the cruel ironies of this new business model is that, in some countries, the role of pension funds is outstanding in the provision of endowments for private equity funds.

3.2.5. Further Reading

1. Backhouse, R. E., & Bateman, B.W. (2011). *Capitalist Revolutionary: John Maynard Keynes*. Cambridge, MA: Harvard University Press.
2. Barnett, V. (2013). *John Maynard Keynes*. London: Routledge, 2013.
3. *Bateman, Bradley (2010). The Return to Keynes.* Cambridge, MA: Harvard University Press.
4. Chick, V. (1983). *Macroeconomics after Keynes*. Deddington: Philip Allan.
5. Davidson, P. (1974). *Money and the Real World.* London: Macmillan.
6. Skidelsky, R.. (1992). *John Maynard Keynes: Hopes Betrayed 1883–1920*; (1994). *The Economist as Saviour 1920–1937*; (2001). *Fighting for Britain 1937–19*46. London: Papermac.
7. Syll, L. P. (2007). *John Maynard Keynes*. Stockholm: SNS Förlag.
8. Temin, P., & Vines, D. (2014). *Keynes: Useful Economics for the World Economy*. Cambridge, MA: MIT Press.

3.3. James Tobin on Bank Money Creation

3.3.1. Setting the Scene

James Tobin is considered to be an Old Keynesian economist. His classic contribution on monetary theory in the early 1960s highlights that, in reality, banks do not have incentives to expand loans and deposits beyond the profitable level. In the article "Commercial Banks as Creators of 'Money' (1963), he shows that credit expansion is the result of profit expectations based on credit demand, costs of backing liabilities and interest-rate spreads between a set of lending and deposit rates. In truth, banks create deposits in the process of lending and hold reserves after evaluating opportunity costs. The main idea of his model of bank creation is that "loans create deposits". In fact, he focuses on the role of banks as financial intermediaries as a special one.

Tobin criticizes mainstream economics and its analysis of the model of money bank creation. In this model, the monetary base (*MB*) is linked to the total stock of money supply (M), that is to say, to the total sum of currency in circulation and demand deposits with banks.

This relation can be represented using the formula $M = m \times MB$, where m, the money multiplier, is higher than one. Its value depends on social decisions about holdings of currency and the participation of legally required and excess bank reserves in total deposits. The money multiplier formula can be represented as $m = (1 + c) / (r + e + c)$, where c is the currency ratio, r is the legally required reserve ratio and e is the excess reserve ratio [11].

In this money multiplier model, commercial banks borrow funds from depositors and make loans to households and businesses. It is supposed that if banks have excess reserves above legal requirements, they will expand loans at a given interest rate. The exogenous increase of reserves on their balance sheets is the starting point of additional loans and deposits.

Tobin dismisses this mainstream money multiplier model of bank creation, acknowledging that loans create deposits. He particularly emphasizes that, among bank strategies, reserve management is a critical one. What Tobin adds to our understanding about the banking system is that banks can turn elastic or inelastic financing conditions as a result of their expectations on liquidity, risks and returns.

The liability composition of banks' financial statements expresses the management of bank reserves. Indeed, commercial banks have a set of liabilities with a variety of maturities, risks, and regulatory requirements. These banks, which have complex portfolios, have to meet the market in order to fundraising deposits, non- deposit borrowings, and wholesale funds in domestic and foreign markets. Thus, reserve management is related to banks' active management of net funds already available for lending and investment as well as the search for additional funds.

Box 17. A biographical note.

James Tobin was born in the city of Champaign, U.S., in 1918. He studied at Harvard where he got his Ph.D. in 1947 and taught Economics in undergraduate and graduate courses at Yale University.
Tobin was director of the Foundation at Yale (1955-1961 and 1964-1965). In the late 1950s, he started writing articles on current economic issues. In the period between 1966 and 1970, he served as Chairman of the New Haven City Plan Commission. However, his main activity in public service was as a Member of President Kennedy's Council of Economic Advisers (1961-62).
In 1981, James Tobin won the Nobel Memorial Prize in Economic Science because of his contributions to macroeconomics and monetary theory, particularly because of his theoretical contribution to the portfolio balance models and the **q** theory of investment.
James Tobin died in 2002 [12].

Box 18. Selected works.

Articles
1958. Liquidity Preference as Behavior Towards Risk
1961. Money, Capital, and Other Stores of Value
1963. Commercial Banks as Creators of 'Money'
1969. A General Equilibrium Approach to Monetary Theory
1975. Keynesian Models of Recession and Depression
1980 Asset Accumulation and Economic Activity.
1981. Money and Finance in the Macro-Economic Process
1982. The Commercial Banking Firm: A Simple Model
1984. On the Efficiency of the Financial System
Books and collected writings
1987. Policies for Prosperity: Essays in a Keynesian Mode
1987-1996. Essays in Economics: v. 1 (1987). Macroeconomics; v. 2 (1987). Consumption and Economics; v. 3 (1987). Theory and Policy; v. 4 (1996). National and International.

In Tobin's framework, commercial banks are not constrained by the previous amount of deposits because banks could be active in fundraising. As a matter of fact, innovative banks promote adjustments of assets and liabilities as a result of expected risks and returns. Their aim is to collect sufficient funds to meet asset growth and earnings targets at acceptable levels of risk. Liability management involves strategies that reveal the banks' ability to refinance their positions without increasing liquidity risks.

3.3.2. Key Concepts

When reading James Tobin, you must remember that:

1. Under the central bank monopoly of issuance, the *monetary base* is a claim that general public, government and banks have on the central bank.
2. The monetary base is considered to be part of the liabilities at the central bank balance sheet in the form of (i) *currency in circulation*, cash hold by public outside the banking system, and (ii) *bank* reserves, cash hold by commercial banks or deposits hold by commercial banks at the central bank (in the form of required and voluntary reserves).
3. Also known as the *monetary base*, the *high powered money* corresponds to notes and coins that perform the payment functions by virtue of legal tender status. The *monetary base* is also called *high-powered money* because of the effects of the *money multiplier* on the quantity of *money supply*.
4. The process of bank money creation involves complex interconnections between central banks' instruments and policies and banks' profit-seeking strategies in the management of their assets and liabilities.

3.3.3. Reading Passages: Money and Finance in the Macro-Economic Process

The Reading Passages presented below were written by James Tobin and were published in his Nobel Prize Lecture *Money and Finance in the Macro-Economic Process,* 1981 [13]. In order to have in-depth understanding of Tobin's contribution, we elaborated a summary of the main ideas.

Reading Passages	***Summary of the Main Ideas***
(...) banks and other financial institutions mediate between borrowers and lenders, making loans to businesses, governments, households, and others, and incurring liabilities to households and other creditors.	*Commercial banks and other financial institutions are financial intermediaries that mete between borrowers and lenders.*
The traditional business of commercial banks is to accept deposits and other obligations payable on demand or at specified times and to acquire assets of less liquidity and longer maturity. Almost all their assets and liabilities, except their owners' equity, are promises to pay currency. Other intermediaries likewise transform their assets into forms better tailored - in convenience of denomination, liquidity, maturity, and risk - to the preferences and circumstances of their creditors. Banks and other intermediaries, together with capital and credit markets, thus create "inside" assets, The traditional business of commercial banks is to accept deposits and other obligations payable on demand or at specified times and to acquire assets of less liquidity and longer maturity. Almost all their assets and liabilities, except their owners' equity, are promises to pay currency. Other intermediaries likewise transform their assets into forms better tailored - in convenience of denomination, liquidity, maturity, and risk - to the preferences and circumstances of their creditors. Banks and other intermediaries, together with capital and credit markets, thus create "inside" assets, claims of agents on each other that wash out in aggregations of privately owned national wealth.	*Commercial banks and other financial intermediaries create inside assets, that is to say, claims of economic agents on each other that turn out to balance in aggregations of private national wealth.*
In particular, banks create inside money, i. e., deposits that serve on a par with government currency as generally acceptable transactions media or as close substitutes therefor, "backed" on the other side of their ledgers not by base money or government debt but by private loans and securities.	*Banks are particular financial intermediaries that create money in the form of deposits.*
(…) the banks' disposable deposits, i. e. deposits net of required reserves, are available for allocation among free reserves, loans, and securities.	*Loans are considered one of the eligible assets of banks.*
Some loans may be rationed at administratively set interest rates, like the "prime", with excess supply from borrowers chronic or frequent.	*Banks can ration loans if they considered they are non-profitable.*

3.3.4. Modern Concerns About Money Supply and Banks' Reserve Management

The interactions between central banks and commercial banks occur in a monetary economy where, according to John Maynard Keynes, money is non–neutral and it is the asset that links the present and the future. Indeed, money is non-neutral in the capital accumulation process that envelops through time.

During the 1980s, the acceptance of Post Keynesian endogenous monetary theory challenged the monetarist earlier attempts to achieve price stability by means of the control of the quantity money supplied through quantitative rules. According to Friedman's (monetarist) understanding of monetary policy, since inflation is ultimately a monetary phenomenon, central banks should directly control their own liabilities, the money supply and the price level. Friedman's theoretical assumptions were founded on empirical evidence that showed a close correlation between the variability of the money supply and the nominal income variability.

Proceeding from the contribution of Tobin to the understanding of money bank creation, Post Keynesian (PK) economics addressed that endogenous money supply is driven by credit [14]. While the PK accommodationist approach points out that the central bank accommodates any increase in bank's demand for reserves due to increasing loans, the PK structuralist approach highlights that the money supply also depends on banks' asset and liability management. What Hyman Minsky's structuralist approach adds to the understanding to the monetary policy challenges is that banks can search for new sources of fundraising as well as make use of the additional reserves at the central bank to make loans. Consequently, the attempt to control the money base puts pressure in the volatility of nominal interest rates.

After the 1980s, in order to avoid this volatility, central banks have privileged the stability of nominal interest rates. Central banks manage nominal interest rates and they can influence the credit market dynamics by affecting the costs of loans and the availability of bank reserves. As a consequence, the monetary base turns out to be a result of complex and multiple decisions and interactions in the economy. As a matter of fact, central bank management can influence credit market features by changing costs and availability of bank reserves. Throughout the economic cycle, any credit expansion turns out to be more elastic if central banks meet the demands of reserves. Indeed, the evolution of money supply is, highly dependent on central banks' reserve management.

However, if central banks refuse to accommodate additional demands for reserves during a boom, banks may introduce financial innovations through expanding interbank loans and asset trading. At the peak of the cycle, central banks act as lenders of last resort to face liquidity constraints.

As a matter of fact, the recent global crisis showed that the central banks´ actions are not independent from private and public pressures. Indeed, since the global financial crisis, monetary policy has been brought to the forefront. Central banks, in the current context of financial liberalization, do not face financial disturbances easily. Indeed, the menace of recession and the shift of investors and banks toward liquid and safe assets, among other factors, have put pressure on central banks and treasuries.

3.3.5. Further Readings

1. Backhouse, R. E., & Boinaovsky, M. (2013). *Transforming Modern Macroeconomics: Exploring Disequilibrium Microfoundations, 1956-2003.* Cambridge, UK: Cambridge University Press.
2. Brainard, W.C. (Ed.) (1991), *Money, Macroeconomics, and Economic Policy: Essays in Honor of James Tobin*, Cambridge, MA: MIT Press.
3. Colander, D. (1999). Conversations with James Tobin and Robert Shiller on the "Yale Tradition" in Macroeconomics. *Macroeconomic Dynamics,* 3(1), 116-143.
4. Dimand, R. W. (2010). Tobin's Keynesianism. In B. Bateman, T. Hirai & M. C. Marcuzzo (Eds.). *The Return to Keynes.* Cambridge, MA: Harvard University Press. 94-107.
5. Lucas, R. E. (1981). Tobin and Monetarism: A Review Article. *Journal of Economic Literature,* 19(2), 558-567.
6. Meltzer, A.H. (1989). Tobin on Macroeconomic Policy: A Review Essay. *Journal of Monetary Economics,* 23(1), 159-173.
7. Young, W., & Zilberfarb, B. Z. (Eds.) (2000). *IS-LM and Modern Macroeconomics.* Boston, Dordrecht, and London: Kluwer Academic Publishers.

3.4. Policy Tool: Monetary Aggregates Measurement

The recent bailout of financial systems has put pressure on the central banks' instruments and policies. In this setting, monetary policy goals and instruments have also been put into question. As a result, some policymakers over the world are discussing new monetary measures.

The simple sum money aggregates index supposed that all monetary components contribute with equal weights to the total and, besides, it considers all components as currency perfect substitutes. It has been argued that as the simple sum index does not weigh the components, it does not properly apprehend liquidity and expenditure issues, for instance.

New solutions based on the Divisia index consider both different degrees of asset liquidity and different expenditure weights of the components of an asset portfolio. In the 1980s, William Barnett developed the Divisia index for monetary quantity aggregation [15]. The Divisia monetary measures rely on theories of consumer demand and economic aggregation. It is supposed that:

- Money is regarded as a consumer durable that yields a flow of monetary services
- Assets are held on behalf of the expected flow of monetary services
- The monetary asset's price is measured by the opportunity cost of holding the asset.

The Divisia monetary aggregates index is an index of money supply mainly used in official statistics and central banking. A Divisia index is a measure of money supply that, attaches a weight to each component of the monetary aggregates. Some monetary assets are held primarily for transactions (cash, current account deposits) while others are held as a store of value (short and long-term bonds, securities, shares, *etc.*). In other words, the Divisia index for monetary aggregates aims to separate the transactions function of money from other functions.

The International Monetary Fund has pointed out the technical quality of the Divisia monetary aggregates. However, most central banks continue to mainly take into account and spread information about the simple-sum measures. There are, however, some countries that have considered the Divisia monetary aggregates index:

- The Bank of England's Divisia monetary aggregate index is available for external use;
- The European Central Bank's Divisia monetary aggregates index is only available for internal use;
- The Bank of Japan's Divisia monetary aggregates index has been used in research publication;
- The Divisia monetary measurement approach has also been introduced in the United States, Canada, Australia, China, Israel, and Switzerland.

It is worth remembering that *The Center for Financial Stability* (www.centerforfinancialstability.org/) maintains an online research resources on Divisia monetary aggregation that include evidences for over 40 countries. According to their statistics, the Divisia monetary aggregates compose a nesting of aggregate components:

Divisia M1: It includes the most liquid monetary-asset components, such as currency, travelers' checks, demand deposits and other checkable deposits.

Divisia M2: It includes those components in the Divisia M1 and adds savings deposits, retail money market funds, small time deposits.

Divisia M3: It includes the components of Divisia M2 and adds institutional money market funds, large time deposits and overnight and term repurchase agreements.

Divisia M4: It includes the components of Divisia M3 and adds commercial papers and Treasury bills. This is the broadest available monetary aggregates.

REFERENCES

[1] Garrison RW. Biography of Eugen von Böhm-Bawerk (1851-1914) 2011. Retrieved from: http://mises.org/about/3229

[2] Böhm-Bawerk E. The positive theory of capital 1889. Retrieved from: ia800200.us.archive.org/31/items/PositiveTheoryOfCapital/PositiveTheoryOfCapital.pdf

[3] Hannoun H. Ultra-low or negative interest rates: What they mean for financial stability and growth 2015.; Eggertsson GB. Liquidity trap. In: Durlauf SN, Blume LE, Eds. The New Palgrave Dictionary of Economics. 2nd ed., UK: Palgrave MacMillan 2008. [http://dx.doi.org/10.1057/978-1-349-95121-5_2482-1]

[4] Backhouse R, Bateman B, Eds. The Cambridge Companion to Keynes. Cambridge: Cambridge University Press 2006. [http://dx.doi.org/10.1017/CCOL0521840902]

[5] Pigou AC. The Theory of Unemployment. London: MacMillan and Co 1933.

[6] Skidelsky R. John Maynard Keynes: 1883-1946: Economist, Philosopher, Statesman. London: Pinguin Books 2004.

[7] Keynes JM. The General Theory of Employment, Interest and Money 1936. Retrieved from: https://www.marxists.org/reference/subject/economics/keynes/general-theory/

[8] International Union of Food. Agricultural, Hotel, Restaurant, Catering, Tobacco and Allied Workers′ Association.IUF . 2007. Retrieved from: http://www.iuf.org/w/sites/default/files/2007%-20A%20Workers'%20Guide%20to%20Private%20Equity%20Buyouts.pdf

[9] Gonçalves JR, Madi MA. Private equity investment and labour: faceless capital and the challenges to trade unions in Brazil. In: Serrano M, Xhafa E, Fichte M, Eds. Trade unions and the global crisis: Labour's visions, strategies and responses. Geneve: Intenational Labour Office 2011.

[10] Bauman Z. Liquid Modernity. U.S.: Polity Press 2000.

[11] Madi MA. 2015. High-powered money. L-P. Rochon,& S. Rossi (Eds.). The Encyclopedia of Central Banking. Cheltenham, UK and Northhampton, MA: Edward Elgar

[12] Media Nobel. James Tobin - Biographical 2014. Retrieved from: http://www.nobelprize.org/nobel_prizes/economic-sciences/laureates/1981/tobin-bio.htmlDimand, R. W. (2014). James Tobin and Modern Monetary Theory. Retrieved from ope.econ.duke.edu/sites/hope.econ.duke.edu/files/TOBIN%20AND%20MODERN%20MONETARY%20THEORY.pdf

[13] Tobin J. Money and Finance in the Macro-Economic Process 1981. Retrieved from: http://nobelprize.org/nobel_prizes/economics/laureates/1981/tobin-lecture.pdf

[14] Madi MA. Monetary Policy Instruments. 2015. In L-P. Rochon & S. Rossi (Eds.). *The Encyclopedia of Central Banking.* Cheltenham, UK and Northhampton, MA: Edward Elgar.; Gnos, C., & Rochon, L-P. (Eds.) (2005). *Post Keynesian principles of economic policy.* Cheltenham, UK and Northhampton, MA: Edward Elgar.

[15] Barnett W A. 1980. Economic Monetary Aggregates: An Application of Index Number and Aggregation Theory. *Journal of Econometrics,* 14(1), 11-48.; Barnett, W. A. (2012). *Getting It Wrong: How Faulty Monetary Statistics Undermine the Fed, the Financial System, and the Economy.* Cambridge and London: MIT Press.

CHAPTER 4

Prices

Abstract: This chapter presents the contributions of Alfred Marshall, Joan Robinson and Milton Friedman to the study of prices. Firstly, Marshall highlighted the forces that shape the perfect markets and its prices. Secondly, Robinson considered the dynamics of real-world markets where imperfect competition seems to dominate. She showed how imperfect competition affects pricing and strategic decision making. Finally, Milton Friedman presented an analysis of inflation that restates the relevance of the quantity theory of money to explain the roots of inflation. His approach to the trade-off between inflation and unemployment has had deep consequences in the neoliberal economic policy agenda.

Keywords: Perfect markets, Imperfect competition, Price stability.

4. INTRODUCTION

Different perspectives from economic thinking are introduced throughout this chapter in order to present insightful perspectives oriented to understand contemporary debates over the challenges to perfect market competition and to the maintenance of price stability. In this attempt, we present the contribution of Alfred Marshall, Joan Robinson and Milton Friedman to the study of prices.

Firstly, Alfred Marshall highlighted the forces that shape the perfect markets and its prices. His economic analysis of markets, firms and industries focuses on the main economic features of the organization of production, behaviour of consumers, competition among firms and market forces toward price and output equilibrium.

Secondly, Joan Robinson considered the dynamics of real-world markets where imperfect competition seems to dominate. She showed how imperfect competition affects pricing and strategic decision making. Managerial decisions include price discrimination and market segmentation, for instance, as practices aimed to increase market share and profits. Both Marshall and Robinson microeconomic studies wonder how the behaviour of consumers and the firms' strategies shape the evolution of prices and output in different industries both in the short and in the long-run.

Maria Alejandra Madi

Finally, Milton Friedman presented an analysis of inflation that is integrated into a macroeconomic framework that restates the relevance of the quantity theory of money and elaborates a theory of money demand to explain the roots of inflation. Considering the price dynamics, his macroeconomic approach highlights not only money supply at the roots of inflation but also the influence of inflation on the short-run and long-run levels of domestic product and employment. His approach to the trade-off between inflation and unemployment deeply influenced the economic policy agenda in the context of neoliberalism.

4.1. Alfred Marshall on the Market Forces

4.1.1. Setting the Scene

According to Alfred Marshall, the narrowness of the works of his contemporary English economists relies on the fact that they used to ignore history and statistics, but that they assigned universality to economic dogmas and paid little attention to study economic variations in habits and institutions of industry.

Marshall addressed that Economics is the study of human beings that aims to explain the ordinary business of life oriented to the satisfaction of their needs. In his *Principles of Economics* (1890), he considered not only induction and deduction as useful methods for Economics, but also the method of partial equilibrium that relies on the idea that it is better to focus the economic analysis about the forces that directly influence a phenomenon and consider the set of other forces in action as *ceteris paribus*, that is to say, consider the other forces as remaining equal during this analysis. According to Joh Maynard Keynes, Marshall is the founder of modern diagrammatic economics in his attempt to describe the market forces in the analysis of the economic phenomena.

Within perfect competition, the price of a good (or commodity) is fixed in the market by the interaction of the forces of its supply and demand. Marshall's demand theory examines how rational consumers behave if they want to maximize their satisfaction from the consumption of goods. The curve of individual demand relates the quantities demanded of a good at certain prices, other things remaining constant. According to the law of diminishing marginal utility, the additional utility (or benefit) that a consumer obtains from an increase in the amount consumed of a good diminishes on behalf of the amount of this good that the consumer already has. Considering the aggregation of the consumers' behaviour in a specific market, the individual demand curves can be aggregated in order to derive the market demand curve that relates the total quantity demanded of a good at certain prices. Rational consumers will substitute one good for another until they get maximum satisfaction.

The price elasticity of demand of a good is the measure of the relationship between a change in the level of a good price and the quantity demanded of this good in a period of time. Among the factors that condition the price elasticity of demand, Marshall highlights the kind and uses of goods, the consumers' preferences and behaviour in terms of habits, the possibility of good substitution and the role of time in shaping demand conditions of a good.

In his *Principles*, Marshall also developed a theory of supply where the rational producer aims at minimizing costs. Costs are classified into; i) prime costs such as wages and raw materials that vary in accordance with the level of production and ii) supplementary costs such as fixed costs related to depreciation expenses, debt services, rental payments and salaries for employees. Among the factors of production, labour is a primary one and the organization of the production in the firms by businessmen is considered to be a kind of labour. Under the marginal productivity theory of distribution, the price of a factor of production depends on its marginal productivity.

Marginal costs in manufacturing follow the law of diminishing returns. In accordance with this economic law, since no improvements are introduced in the cultivation of land, if more units of capital and labour are added in land cultivation, this fact generally results in less than proportionate increases in the total quantity produced. Considering the law of diminishing returns in manufacturing, as the quantity of labour added to fixed capital increases in the short-term, there are less than proportionate increases in the total quantity produced and the marginal costs of production generally rises.

Marshall's introduction of the relevance of time in the study of the markets represented a significant contribution to microeconomic analysis, both in the short but also in the long-run. Considering the long-term analysis of industries, Marshall highlights an industry would produce more cheaply in the presence of increasing returns. Indeed, the long-run supply curve of an industry is related to the behaviour of internal and external economies of scale. First, internal economies of scale are related to the kind of business organization and the level of efficiency of the firm. They usually increase along with the increases in the production levels. Second, external economies depend on system factors that are external to a firm. They usually affect the evolution of the costs of production along with the expansion of the size of the industry.

Among the internal economies, Marshall points out the economy of the utilization of materials, the efficiency of investing in larger machines, the reduction in costs on behalf of discounts for purchasing and selling in huge quantity, and for low freights, the easier loan conditions, the improvements in skills, specialization of tasks and division of labour. Smaller manufacturing firms have difficulties in achieving some kinds of internal economies. They are, indeed, more common in large business. Due to the long-term evolution of internal economies, average costs decrease as the level of output increases. However, average costs could rise after achieving a certain level of output on behalf of the lack of management skills and of the emergence of marketing challenges. As a result, the long-run evolution of internal economies and diseconomies of scale happen to condition the U-shaped average cost curve.

When studying the external economies to the firm and the internal economies to the industry, Marshall considers the economies of localization that refer to the main features of the environment of the firms in an industry. Among the economies of localization, he highlights the linkages between industries and the access to technology, knowledge and skilled labour. External economies are responsible for producing under decreasing costs in the industry. In the context of perfect competition, the representative firm refers to a firm that benefits from internal and external economies and obtains fair performance - it is considered an average firm.

In 1895, Marshall's inaugural lecture at Cambridge highlighted that Economics is conditioned by constant and rapid changing conditions of ordinary business life. In his opinion, each generation is due to the discovery the circumstances and changes that affect business and livelihoods. Marshall's overriding motivation for doing economics was his interest in understanding current business features and social issues. For him, economic theory is not worthy if it does not move in the direction of conclusions that could be useful in practice to address economic problems. This attempt requires a deep knowledge of the real-world facts in all sectors of economic activity.

Box 19. A biographical note.

Alfred Marshall was born in the city of Clapham, United Kingdom, in the year of 1842 within a family with Christian morals. Under this influence, he developed throughout all his life concerns with poverty, labour issues and human rights In the undergraduate studies at the University of Cambridge, he revealed a preference for mathematics. At that time, great controversies on Christian theology, metaphysical agnosticism, evolutionary progress, and utilitarian ethics dominated the English academic setting. After taking his degree in 1865, Marshall began studies on metaphysics, ethics and social sciences. After studying Ethics, he developed his interest in Economics and became a lecturer of Moral Sciences.

In January 1885, he returned at Cambridge, where he taught Political Economy. There was an interruption in this position due to a membership in the Royal Commission on Labour in the period between 1891 and 1894.

Throughout twenty-three years as professor, he was a cofounder of the School of Economics at the University of Cambridge and of the British Economic Association (today Royal Economic Society). He also participated in the Women's Degrees Controversy in Cambridge and in the design of the Cambridge Economics Tripos.

He remained in Cambridge until his resignation in 1908. Before his eighty-second birthday, he died in 1924 [1].

Arthur Pigou, Joan Robinson and Francis Edgeworth, among some prominent disciples, developed Marshall's legacy and expanded his ideas in different ways. It was Joan Robinson the economist that turned out to develop a theoretical approach to the economics of imperfect competition from Marshall's commentaries on special features of the markets.

Box 20. Selected works.

Books
1890. Principles of Economics
1892. Elements of the Economics of Industry
1903. The new Cambridge curriculum in Economics and associated branches of Political Science: its purpose and plan
1919. Industry and Trade: A Study of Industrial Technique and Business Organization
1923. Money, Credit and Commerce
Other papers and collected writings
1906. Introduction to the Tripos in economics and associated branches of political science
1842-1924. Official papers of Alfred Marshall: a supplement
1925. Memorials of Alfred Marshall
1975. The early economic writings

4.1.2. Key Concepts

When reading Alfred Marshall, you must remember that:

1. In a perfect market, the price (value) of any good is fixed at the equilibrium point of its supply and demand.
2. In a perfect market, the prices of goods are fixed by the economic forces that condition the behaviour of their supply and demand. The behaviour of the marginal utility of a good and of its marginal cost of production is decisive to apprehend the forces beyond the evolution of good prices.
3. Time and space are relevant analytical elements in the study of the evolution of market prices.
4. Considering the role of time in perfect markets: (i) when the supply of the firm is fixed, the market price of a good mainly depends on the conditions of demand; (ii) in the short-run, as the amount of variable inputs can change and the scale of the plants remains fixed, prices can be affected by the level of production in the industry.; (iii) in the long-run, changes in both the amount of variable inputs and in the size and features of plants can affect the evolution of market prices.

4.1.3. Reading Passages: On Markets

The Reading Passages presented below were written by Alfred Marshall and were published in the book *Principles of Economics*, Book V, Chapter 1, 1890 [2]. In order to have in-depth understanding of Marshall's contribution, we elaborated a summary of the main ideas.

Reading Passages	*Summary of the Main Ideas*
We have now to examine the general relations of demand and supply; especially those which are connected with that adjustment of price, by which they are maintained in "equilibrium."	*The adjustment of the market price of a good depends on the general relations of demand and supply.*
Thus the more nearly perfect a market is, the stronger is the tendency for the same price to be paid for the same thing at the same time in all parts of the market: but of course if the market is large, allowance must be made for the expense of delivering the goods to different purchasers; each of whom must be supposed to pay in addition to the market price a special charge on account of delivery.	*Under perfect competition, there is a trend for the same price to be paid in all parts of the market.*
There are many special causes which may widen or narrow the market of any particular commodity: but nearly all those things for which there is a very wide market are in universal demand, and capable of being easily and exactly described. Thus for instance cotton, wheat, and iron satisfy wants that are urgent and nearly universal. They can be easily described, so that they can be bought and sold by persons at a distance from one another and at a distance also from the commodities	*Space affects the market forces of supply and demand*
Again, markets vary with regard to the period of time which is allowed to the forces of demand and supply to bring themselves into equilibrium with one another, as well as with regard to the area over which they extend.	*Time also affects the market forces of supply and demand.*
And this element of Time requires more careful attention just now than does that of Space. For the nature of the equilibrium itself, and that of the causes by which it is determined, depend on the length of the period over which the market is taken to extend.	*The adjustment of prices towards equilibrium depends on the period of extension of the market.*
We shall find that if the period is short, the supply is limited to the stores which happen to be at hand: if the period is longer, the supply will be influenced, more or less, by the cost of producing the commodity in question; the stock available at the time for sale in the market; so that it cannot be directly influenced by the cost of production.	*In the short-run, the supply of a good is limited to the stock available for sale in the market. The supply cannot be directly influenced by the costs of production.*
(…) if the period is very long, this cost will in its turn be influenced, more or less, by the cost of producing the labour and the material things required for producing the commodity.	*In the long-run, the supply of a good can vary on behalf of the possibility of its increasing production. The supply is directly influenced by the costs of production of labour and other inputs.*

4.1.4. Modern Concerns About Competition Policies

Although Alfred Marshall realized that some features of the markets prevent achieving the free market equilibrium, he did not recommend the adoption of a law-based competition policy [3]. However, competition policies' relevance has increased among public policies in the 20th century.

Among the recent changes in the contemporary economic setting, the restructure of manufacturing and services has fostered the formation of global networks of production. These transformations have affected in asymmetrical ways corporations and consumers and they enhance a serious rethinking of the market dynamics and market power issues.

Competition policies must prevent or correct anti-competitive behavior [4]. To achieve these targets, the National Competition Authorities usually monitor:

- The agreements between firms that limit competition, such as cartels or other arrangements, in which firms agree to avoid competition in particular markets by setting their own rules;
- The emergence of abuse of a dominant position where a firm act as a major player in a particular market to reduce the number of competitors;
- The occurrence of mergers and other permanent or temporary agreements between firms that mainly aim at increase profits at the expense of increasing the benefits to consumers;
- The evolution of the cooperation with other competition authorities on behalf of the global expansion of firms.

These competition policies aim to apply rules to commit companies to fair competition. As a result, it is expected that these policies should enhance higher business efficiency, price reduction, product quality improvement and wider choices for consumers. In other words, it is supposed that consumers should be the beneficiaries of these public interventions.

4.1.5. Further Reading

1. Cook, S.J. (2009). *The intellectual foundations of Alfred Marshall's economic science. A rounded globe of knowledge.* Cambridge: Cambridge University Press.
2. Hart, N. (2013). *Alfred Marshall and Modern Economics. Equilibrium Theory and Evolutionary Economics*. Houndmills: Palgrave MacMillan.
3. McWilliams-Tullberg, R. (Ed.) (1990). *Alfred Marshall in Retrospect.* Aldershot: Edward Raffaelli, T. (2003). Marshall's evolutionary economics,

London and New York: Routledge.
4. Pigou. A. C. (1953). *Alfred Marshall and Current Th*ought. London: MacMillan.
5. Whitaker, J.K. (Ed) (1996). *The correspondence of Alfred Marshall, Economist.* 3 volumes. Cambridge: Cambridge University Press.
6. Wood, J. C. (2004). *Alfred Marshall: Critical Asse*ssments. London: Routledge.

4.2. Joan Robinson on Imperfect Competition

4.2.1. Setting the Scene

Joan Robinson was one the greatest economist woman in England in the 20th century that defended the non-neutrality of economic science. She highlighted the need to distinguish the different roles of *logical* and *historical* time in economic analysis.

Both Alfred Marshall and Joan Robinson studied microeconomic topics such as the firms' strategies of production and pricing, the monopolistic and competitive features of the markets and the role of the behaviour of consumers in shaping the price dynamics. Robinson's first major book was *The Economics of Imperfect Competition* that was published in 1933- the same year when the British economist Edward Chamberlin also published his book *The Theory of Monopolistic Competition*. However, their approaches to the markets differed in several aspects [5].

Her aim was to show the challenges for building a theory of value and distribution that considers either perfect competition or perfect monopoly as assumptions. Robinson restates the Marshallian contribution to price theory so as to examine the outcomes of imperfect competition. In her understanding, the case of perfect competition is very special. In perfect markets, all consumers should have the same preferences and, at any one time, each consumer should deal with only one firm. As a result, if the price of one firm is increased, this fact would provoke the total loss of its sales if the prices of other firms remained the same.

The first prerequisite of perfect competition is that the good should be clearly delimited from other goods, that is to say, the characterization of a perfect market depends on the clear demarcation of the commodity that is sold and bought. In particular, she examines how strategies of price discrimination and market segmentation influence the price elasticity of the demand curve of the individual firm and the market equilibrium. Indeed, perfect competition will be reduced on behalf of a lower price elasticity of the demand curve. Indeed, the price elasticity of the demand curve of a good reveals the market competition features.

Considering the markets where imperfect competition dominates, Robinson starts the analysis with a single firm in an industry. She clarifies that the market is considered imperfect when consumers have different scales of preferences between firms that produce the same good. As a result, imperfect competition in this market affects the price elasticity of the demand curve of an individual firm and of the industry. Besides, the challenges for equalizing the price and the marginal cost in imperfect markets is due to the fact that in those markets the firms' supply curves could reveal increasing, decreasing, or constant costs.

Imperfect market competition will also arise when the participation of one firm's output in the total output of the industry is high. In this case, a raise in this firm's output could change the output of the industry and this fact may result in relevant changes in the good price.

According to Robinson's approach, empirical evidences show that imperfect competition is usually associated with the search for high level of normal profits. In this attempt, managerial decisions include price discrimination and market segmentation, for instance, as practices aimed to increase market share and profits.

Within the markets and industries, old-established firms take advantage of a *good will* to influence the market price and to set high entry costs to potential rivals. Consequently, the market power of these firms turns out to reinforce unfair competition.

Box 21. A biographical note.

Joan Robinson was born at Camberley, Surrey, in 1903. In 1922, she began her studies at the University of Cambridge, where Alfred Marshall and Arthur Pigou were dominant at that time. After graduating in economics, she married Professor Sir Austin Robinson and spent two years in India.

After their return to England, they settled in Cambridge for their all lives. In the early 1930s, she took part of the "Cambridge Circus" – a group of economists that discussed the drafts of Keynes's *General Theory*. This group included Richard Kahn, Piero Sraffa, Roy Harrod, James Meade and Austin Robinson. Later in the 1930s, the meeting with Michal Kalecki led her to rethink her understanding of the Marxian theory. Some years later, after having joined the British Academy (1958), Robinson became a fellow of Newnham College (1962), full professor and fellow of Girton College (1965) and the first female fellow of King's College (1979). At that time, she was also interested in the challenges of underdeveloped and developing countries and published a book on China.

Towards the late 1970s, her research was mainly concentrated on methodological issues in Economics. She also turned out to be very disappointed with the paths of development in economic theory.

At the beginning of 1983, she suffered a stroke from which she never recovered. She died six months later [6].

Box 22. Selected works.

Books
1932. Economics as a Serious Subject. The Apologia of an Economist to the Mathematician, the Scientists and the Plain Man
1933. The Economics of Imperfect Competition
1937. Introduction to the Theory of Employment.
1937. Essays in the Theory of Employment
1956. The Accumulation of Capital
1960. Exercises in Economic Analysis
1962. Economic Philosophy
1966. Economics: An Awkward Corner
1971. Economic Heresies
1978. Contributions to Modern Economics
1979. Aspects of Development and Underdevelopment
1980. What Are the Questions? And Other Essays
Collected writings
1951-80. Collected Economic Papers

4.2.2. Key Concepts

When reading Joan Robinson, you must remember that:

1. A market is considered imperfect when consumers have different scales of preferences between firms that produce the same good. Under imperfect competition, the demand curve for a good of an individual firm slopes downward. Besides, good price is higher than the marginal revenue because of the price inelasticity of demand.
2. Imperfect market competition will also arise when the participation of a firm's level of production in the total industry's output is high.
3. Normal profits refer to the level of profits got by firms when no changes in the number of firms occur in an industry. When the level of profits is higher than the normal level, new firms will be stimulated to enter the market.
4. In imperfect markets, managerial decisions are practices aimed to increase market share and profits that include price discrimination and market segmentation.

4.2.3. Reading Passages: What is Perfect Competition

The Reading Passages presented below were written by Joan Robinson and were published in the article *What is Perfect Competition?,* 1954 [7]. In order to have in-depth understanding of Robinson's contribution, we elaborated a summary of the main ideas.

Reading Passages	*Summary of the Main Ideas*
The idea that there is one level of profits which obtains in competitive industries, and that when competition is not perfect profits must exceed this level, is clearly untenable.	*Normal profits are not necessarily uniform in the real-world industries.*
For the market to be perfect it is necessary first that all buyers should be alike in respect to preferences, and second that each buyer should deal with only one firm at any one time. When these conditions are fulfilled a rise in the price charged by any one firm would, if other prices remained the same, lead to a complete cessation of its sales. And this is the criterion of a perfect market.	*According to the criterion of a perfect market, all buyers should have the same preferences and each buyer should deal with only one firm at any one time.*
Competition will be more perfect the smaller is the ratio of the output of one firm to the output of the industry, and more perfect the greater is the elasticity of the total demand curve.	*The perfect elasticity of demand is a necessary condition for perfect competition*
For the form of the demand curve represents the degree of competition between the product of this industry and other commodities. The stronger the competition from substitutes for this commodity the smaller the degree of competition within the industry necessary to secure any given elasticity of demand for each separate producer.	*The form of the demand curve is relevant to characterize the perfect market.*
If competition is absolutely perfectly perfect an increase in the output of one firm by one unit would leave the output of the industry unchanged and there would be no change in price at all. Competition will be near enough to perfection for practical purposes if an increase in the output of one firm by one unit increases the output of the industry by so much less than one unit that the effect upon price is negligible.	*If one firm increases its production by one unit in a perfect market, the market price and the output of other firms will not change.*
We have thus reached the conclusion that there is not one universal value for the "large number of firms" which ensures perfect competition.4 In each particular case, with given slopes of the marginal cost curves, there is a certain definite number of firms which will produce competition of an agreed degree of perfection, and this number, in some cases, may be quite small.	*The number of firms selling in a perfect market is a certain definite one.*

4.2.4. Modern Concerns About Global Markets and Economic Actors

Current investment chains are characterized by cross-investments among institutional investors, outsourcing of ownership and asset management functions and complexity in equity market structure and trade practices. In this setting, the wealth and power of investors whose assets are embodied in financial assets (securities, bonds, shares, *etc.*) have increased. Meanwhile, financial firms have increasingly dominated firm groups.

The expansion of the organization of production across nation-states has been a reality since the mid-1950s. The existence of nation-states with different regulatory regimes in labour markets, social security, financial and fiscal regulations have created opportunities for specific strategies offered by transnationality.

Considering this background, who are the key economic actors that hold the largest fraction of control in the global setting? To what extent are the top economic global actors interconnected with each other?

To answer these questions, James Glattfelder develops an analysis of the global ownership network of Transnational Corporations (TNCs) in his 2012 book *Decoding Complexity: Uncovering Patterns in Economic Networks* [8]. As a result of a deep analysis, the author uncovers the true organization of key global actors and describes features of the complex systems of current real-world ownership networks. His attempt lies at the interface between economics and the emerging field referred to as complexity science. Among the research conclusions, he lists the top 50 corporate power-holders considering that the importance of the economic actors is related to their level of integrated control. As a matter of fact, the top economic actors organize a global network of corporations and are highly interconnected. Most of the top power-holders are financial intermediaries.

From an economics point of view, the current global business reality has relevant implications on the evolution of the features of market competition. The current global network of cross-ownership and cross-investment shapes a global set of interactions that require a systemic analysis of market competition. Indeed, corporations and their power-holders have increasing influence on the evolution of prices, production and investment in local economies [9]. As Robinson warned, the evolution of imperfect competition has direct effects on prices, output and, therefore, affect the consumers.

Indeed, the density of the interconnections between the financial and non-financial companies in the context of this power and control's network backbone exposes the local economies to new market risks. As the interest of global companies does not generally coincide with the interests of local societies, these risks need to be faced with new anti-trust practices and new rules on cross-ownerships and cross-investments.

4.2.5. Further Reading

1. Cicarelli, J., & Cicarelli, J (2004). *Distinguished Women Economists*. Westport, CT: Greenwood Press.
2. Gibson, B. (Ed.) (2005). *Joan Robinson's Economics. A Centennial Celebration*. Cheltenham, UK: Edward Elgar
3. Marcuzzo, M. C. (2003). Joan Robinson and the Three Cambridge Revolutions,

Review of Political Economy, 15 (4), 545-60.
4. Marcuzzo, M. C., & Rosselli, A. (Eds.) (2005), *Economists in Cambridge: A Study through their Correspondence, 1907-1946*. London: Routledge.
5. Marcuzzo, M. C., Pasinetti, L., & Roncaglia, A. (Eds.) (1996). *The Economics of Joan Robinson.* London and New York: Routledge.
6. Aslanbeigui, N. & Oakes, G. (2009). *The Provocative Joan Robinson: The Making of a Cambridge Economist*. Durham: Duke University Press
7. Samuelson, P.A. (1967). The monopolistic competition revolution. In R. M. Kuenne (Ed.) *Monopolistic Competition Theory: Studies in Impact. Essays in honour of Edward H. Chamberlin*. New York: Wiley & Sons.
8. Turner, M. S. (1989). *Joan Robinson and the Americans*. Armonk, N.Y.: M.E. Sharpe.

4.3. Milton Friedman on Inflation as a Monetary Process

4.3.1. Setting the Scene

Milton Friedman´s contribution to the inflationary challenges in capitalist economies is at the centre of the transformations of the international order in the late 1960s. His on the free markets have highlighted the importance of price stability to achieve economic growth. Indeed, after the 1960s, his influence on the school of thought called monetarism as a restatement of the quantity theory of money was relevant not only in American academic debates but also in the policy making process. Since then, the debate around the causes of inflation has been intense between monetarists and post Keynesians.

Friedman's positive economics restates the relevance of self-regulated markets as he defends the market price system as a social organizer mechanism. He argues that market flexibility, that is to say, the elimination of restrictions both at the international and the domestic levels, would guarantee stability and equilibrium in all markets. Market equilibrium would result from rational choices of economic agents.

Friedman's reformulation of the quantity theory of money replaces the Irving Fisher's transaction form of the equation, $M.V = P.Q$, where M is the stock of money supply, V is the circulation velocity of money, P is the aggregate price level and Q is the level of aggregate real output.

Friedman proposes an income form of this equation, $M.V = P.y$, where where M is the stock of money supply, V is the income velocity of money, P is the aggregate price level and y is the level of aggregate real output.

Indeed, the monetarist approach to the quantity theory of money is founded on the empirical evidence that shows a close correlation between variations in money supply, nominal aggregate income and prices. In this theoretical approach, the quantity theory is mainly a theory of money demand and it is connected and integrated into the price theory within the framework of general equilibrium.

Money demand is related to i) permanent income and total wealth (bonds, equities, money, human capital and physical goods); ii) the composition of total wealth between human capital and other assets; iii) the expected future return rates on monetary and non-monetary assets; iv) other variables, such as tastes and preferences. Friedman states that the demand for nominal money balances is a stable function of the above variables and that the income velocity of money (V) is also stable. As V is stable, there is a stable relation between nominal balances and nominal gross domestic product. Therefore, other things being equal, money demand and permanent income are positively related.

For Friedman, inflation is a monetary phenomenon and price instability results from the wrong economic policies to finance government spending or to increase short-term employment and gross domestic product. As central banks adopt expansionary monetary policies to stimulate domestic income, this monetary expansion turns out to foster inflation since money demand is stable in relation to nominal income. Any increase in the money supply causes a divergence between actual and desired nominal balances.

After an increase in the stock of money supply, the economic agents would adjust their new levels of money balances to the desired level of money balances by buying new goods, services and financial assets. As the result of the portfolio adjustment process, short-run increases in the levels of spending, real output and market prices are observed. However, only the market prices are permanently affected in the long-run.

Considering this background for explaining the inflationary pressures in advanced economies in the late 1960s, Friedman blamed Keynesian aggregate demand policies to have provoked price instability and stagnation. In the monetarist view, discretionary monetary policy explains short-run cyclical fluctuations. As for Friedman, inflation is understood to be a monetary phenomenon, central banks should adopt a rule of monetary policy to manage the stock of money supply and, therefore, to control the evolution of the general price level.

Friedman's interpretation of the Phillips curve highlights its negative slope in the short-run as a result of his analysis about the outcomes of unanticipated inflation by workers and employers. Indeed, expansionary monetary policies can temporarily stimulate the levels of employment and output because of the misinterpretation of the market information by workers and employers. However, the long-run Phillips curve is vertical at the natural rate of unemployment because money is neutral in relation to real output.

Considering the Nobel Prize lecture *Inflation and Unemployment* (1976), Friedman's approach to the Phillips curve trade-off between inflation and unemployment enhances a critique on the active role of central banks in managing interest rates to achieve higher employment or real gross domestic product growth as ultimate targets.

Box 23. A biographical note.

Milton Friedman was born in 1912, in New York, United States. After attending public elementary and secondary schools, he studied at Rutgers University (1932) where he got a major in Mathematics and Economics. He concluded his doctoral dissertation at the University of Columbia and, since that time, his wife Rose turned out to be coauthor in some publications. In the mid 1940s, he became professor at the University of Chicago Economics Department and worked as a researcher at the National Bureau of Economic Research where he and Anna Schwartz developed research projects on monetary history and statistics. After his retirement in 1975, Friedman received in the year of 1976 the Nobel Prize in Economics. Later on, he continued to be active in public policy and became an adviser to Ronald Reagan's campaign (1980) and, after the election, became advisor of the President on economic policy. He was awarded the National Medal of Science in the year of 1988 and ten years before his death he established The Milton and Rose D. Friedman Foundation. He died in 2006 [10].

Box 24. Selected works.

Articles 1948. A Monetary and Fiscal Framework for Economic Stability 1951. Some Comments on the Significance of Labour Unions for Economic Policy 1953. Economic Advice and Political Limitations: Rejoinder 1952. Price, Income, and Monetary Changes in Three Wartime Period 1959. The Demand for Money: Some Theoretical and Empirical Results 1961. The Lag in Effect of Monetary Policy *Books* 1953. Essays in Positive Economics 1956. The Quantity Theory of Money –A Restatement‖ in Studies in the Quantity Theory of Money 1957. A theory of the consumption function 1962. Price Theory, a Provisional Text. 1962. Capitalism and Freedom 1963. A Monetary History of the United States, 1867-1960

Friedman recommends that the target of monetary policy should be price stability and, when possible, central banks should follow a zero inflation rate. He suggests the adoption of the quantitative control of the monetary base as the optimal monetary policy instrument to stabilize prices. In open economies, he adds the adoption of flexible exchange rates in conjunction with the quantitative control of the monetary base to obtain price stability. Flexible exchange rates would permit the achievement of general equilibrium if domestic prices would adjust to costs. To stabilize prices, each country would take care of its monetary policy and leave to the market the determination of exchange rates.

4.3.2. Key Concepts

When reading Milton Friedman, you must remember that:

1. Central Banks should follow monetary rules to avoid inflation.
2. The money demand and supply equation is indicated $Ms = Md$, where Ms is the money supply and Md is money demand. It defines the quantity of money of equilibrium.
3. The Phillips curve shows the relation between unemployment and the rate of change of nominal wages (or prices). This relation is negative in the short-run.
4. The non-accelerating inflation rate of unemployment (NAIRU) refers to the level of unemployment that does not put upward pressures on inflation. This level is conditioned by the behaviour of real factors of the economy.

4.3.3. Reading Passages: Inflation and Unemployment

The Reading Passages presented below were written by Milton Friedman and were published in his Nobel Prize Lecture *Inflation and Unemployment,* 1976 [11]. In order to have in-depth understanding of Friedman's contribution, we elaborated a summary of the main ideas.

Reading Passages	***Summary of the Main Ideas***
In both social and natural sciences, the body of positive knowledge grows by the failure of a tentative hypothesis to predict phenomena the hypothesis professes to explain; by the patching up of that hypothesis until someone suggests a new hypothesis that more elegantly or simply embodies the troublesome phenomena, and so on ad infinitum. In both, experiment is sometimes possible, sometimes not (witness meteorology). In both, no experiment is ever completely controlled, and experience often offers evidence that is the equivalent of controlled experiment. In both, there is no way to have a self-contained closed system or to avoid interaction between the observer and the observed.	*Positive knowledge grows in both social and natural sciences.*
Professional controversy about the relation between inflation and unemployment has been intertwined with controversy about the relative role of monetary, fiscal, and other factors in influencing aggregate demand. One issue deals with how a change in aggregate nominal demand, however produced, works itself out through changes in employment and price levels; the other, with the factors accounting for the changes in aggregate nominal demand. The two issues are closely related.	*The study of unemployment has been intertwined with the controversy about the role of aggregate demand policies.*

Contd.....

Reading Passages	*Summary of the Main Ideas*
(...) what matters is not inflation per se, but unanticipated inflation; there is no stable trade-off between inflation and unemployment; there is a "natural rate of unemployment" (UN), which is consistent with the real forces and with -- accurate perceptions; unemployment can be kept below that level only by an accelerating inflation; or above it, only by accelerating deflation. The "natural rate of unemployment", a term I introduced to parallel Knut Wicksell's "natural rate of interest", is not a numerical constant but depends on "real" as opposed to monetary factors - the effectiveness of the labour market, the extent of competition or monopoly, the barriers or encouragements to working in various occupations, and so on.	*The relevant concept is unanticipated inflation because of its effects on the levels of employment, production and prices in the short-run.*
An increased variability of actual or anticipated inflation may raise the natural rate of unemployment in two rather different ways. First, increased volatility shortens the optimum length of unindexed commitments and renders indexing more advantageous. But it takes time for actual practice to adjust (...) A second related effect of increased volatility of inflation is to render market prices a less efficient system for coordinating economic activity.	*Central banks should avoid the variability of the inflation levels because of its deleterious effects on economic efficiency.*
There is a "natural rate of unemployment" at any time determined by real factors (...) The natural-rate hypothesis contains the original Phillips curve hypothesis as a special case and rationalizes a far broader range of experience, in particular the phenomenon of stagflation.	*Real factors determine the natural rate of unemployment.*

4.3.4. Modern Concerns About Price Stability

Since the 1970s, due to Milton Friedman's influence, nation- states reduced and even eliminated barriers to the international movement of money. Neoliberal policies have focused on privatizing state-owned enterprises, liberalizing foreign trade and reducing welfare spending. In addition, the neoliberal agenda has privileged flexible or floating exchange rates, the openness of financial markets and the elimination of controls on capital movements. Beyond these economic policy changes, there is the belief that free markets are inherently stable. From this perspective, macroeconomic instability is the result of wrong economic policy options - mainly of those policies that aim to promote economic growth, job creation and income distribution. In this setting, a low and stable inflation has been widely recognized as the main target of macroeconomic policies.

Looking back, in the early 1980s, many economists and policy makers discussed the role of the monetary policy in price stabilization [12]. On behalf of the recognition that money demand seemed to be less stable than theoretically expected, the interest rate was adopted as the principal monetary policy instrument. Therefore, since then, the management of short-term nominal interest rate has been adopted as the privileged monetary instrument. Within this context, the short-term interest rate is then adjusted to face changes in inflation and output gaps.

Indeed, the adoption of the Taylor rule has changed practices of central banks all around the world. It is worth remembering that the so-called "New Consensus in Macroeconomics" has favoured the management of the short-term interest rate in conjunction with inflation targeting practices [13]. With open capital accounts, the monetary policy, aimed to stabilize prices, subordinates fiscal policy and requires flexible exchange rates or managed floating exchange rates. Increasingly, the Taylor rule turned out to be the new framework of monetary policy on behalf of the consensus built around its empirical success. As a result, inflationary targeting practices emerged in the international economy.

Currently, the central bank's interest rate policy, as the main policy instrument, has been challenged by expectations and the arbitrage/speculation of global investors in the context of the current global financial architecture, where the actions of the US Federal Reserve, at the top of the hierarchy of central banks, strongly affects the price of assets and the composition of global portfolios.

4.3.5. Further Readings

1. Frazer, W. (1988). *Power and Ideas: Milton Friedman and the Big U-Turn.* Gainesville: Gulf Atlantic.
2. Hammond, D. (Ed.) (1999). *The Legacy of Milton Friedman as a Teacher.* Cheltenham: Edward Elgar.
3. Hammond, J.D. (1996). *Theory and Measurement: Causality Issues in Milton Friedman's Monetary Economics.* Cambridge: Cambridge University Press.
4. Hirsch, A., & De Marchi, N. (1990). *Milton Friedman: Economics in Theory and in Practice.* Ann Arbor: University of Michigan Press.
5. Kaldor, N. (1982). *The Scourge of Monetarism.* Oxford: Oxford University Press.
6. Klein, D. (2013). Why Is There No Milton Friedman Today? A Symposium Prologue. *Econ Journal Watch.* 10(2): 157-161.
7. Leeson, R. (Ed) (2003), Keynes, *Chicago and Friedman.* London: Pickering and Chatto.
8. Smithin, J. (2003). *Controversies in Monetary Economics.* Aldershot, UK and Brookfield, US: Edward Elgar.

4.4. Policy tools: Inflation Targeting

Following inflation targeting practices, central banks manage the short-term nominal interest rate to foster price stability [14]. To better understand the inflation targeting as a policy tool, suppose that a central bank chooses an inflation target **π*** and uses the short-term interest rate (open market rate per year) as its main instrument. This central bank will change the current nominal level of the interest rate if:

- Current inflation **π** moves away from target **π***;
- Real **GDP** (Gross Domestic Product) moves away from its potential (**GDP***).

When current inflation diverges from the target inflation rate, or real *GDP* diverges from potential *GDP*, central banks could manage the level of the open market interest rate and smooth out fluctuations of prices. Therefore, following the Taylor rule:

- If real *GDP* is lower than the potential, central banks will lower the short-term interest rate, that is to say, *r (t)* will be lower than *r'*;
- If current inflation increases above the target, central banks will raise the short-term interest rate, that is to say, *r (t)* will be higher than *r'*.

To manage the interest rate according to the inflation targeting practices, central banks may follow the equation below:

$$r(t) = \pi + r' + 0.5 \times (\pi - \pi^*) + 0.5 \times (GDP - GDP^*)$$

Let's consider a numerical example. Suppose that:

- The current short-term interest rate *r'* is 2%, the inflation target is $\pi^* = 2\%$ and the current inflation is $\pi = 3\%$;
- The inflation gap is positive: $\pi - \pi^* = 1\%$ *or* $3\% - 2\%$;
- There is a positive output gap of 1% since real *GDP* is 1% above its potential *GDP**.

In this case, the Taylor rule suggests that, in the period t, the short-term nominal interest rate should be raised upwards. In other words, the central bank may promote an increase in the nominal open market interest rate in order to defeat the inflationary pressures in the short-run.

REFERENCES

[1] Keynes JM. 1924. Alfred Marshall, 1842-19241. *The Economic Journal,* 34 (135), 311-372. ; Whitaker, J. K. (Ed.) (1990). *Centenary essays on Alfred Marshall*, Cambridge: Cambridge University Press.

[2] Marshall A. Principles of Economics 1890. Retrieved from: http://www.econlib.org/library/Marshall/marP.html

[3] Giocoli N. British Economists on Competition Policy (1890-1920) 2012. Retrieved from: https://papers. ssrn.com/sol3/papers2.cfm?abstract_id=2070185

[4] Elhauge E, Geradin D. Global Competition Law and Economics Oxford: Hart Publishing; Whish, R, & Bailey, D (2014) Competition Law Oxford: Oxford Press Dunne, N (2015) Competition Law and Economic Regulation: Making and Managing Markets. Cambridge: Cambridge UP 2011.

[5] Enke S. On Maximizing Profits: A Distinction Between Chamberlin and Robinson. Am Econ Rev 1951; 41(4): 566-78.

[6] Pasinetti LL. Robinson, Joan Violet. In: Eatwell J, Milgate M, Newman P, Eds. The New Palgrave: A Dictionary of Economics. UK: Palgrave Macmillan 1987; Vol. 4: pp. 212-7. [http://dx.doi.org/10.1057/978-1-349-95121-5_1784-1]

[7] Robinson J. What is Perfect Competition? Q J Econ 1934; 49(1): 104-20. [http://dx.doi.org/10.2307/1883878]

[8] Glattfelder J. Decoding Complexity: Uncovering Patterns in Economic Networks. Berlin: Springer-Verlag Berlin Heidelberg 2013. [http://dx.doi.org/10.1007/978-3-642-33424-5]

[9] Ietto-Gillies G. The multinationalságe is everywhere but in the economics curriculum. 2014. In (Eds.) Madi, M. A. C., & Reardon, J. *The economics Curriculum: towards a radical reformulation*. UK: WEA books

[10] Friedman M, Friedman RD. *Two Lucky People*. 1998. Chicago: University of Chicago Press. ; Lindbeck, A (Ed.) (1992) Milton Friedman. Biographical. *Nobel Lectures*. Singapore: World Scientific Publishing Co.

[11] Friedman M. Inflation and Unemployment 1976. Retrieved from: http://www.nobelprize.org/ nobel_prizes/ economic-sciences/laureates/1976/friedman-lecture.html

[12] Kaldor N. The Scourge of Monetarism Oxford: Oxford University Press Karier, T (1997) Great Experiments in American Economic Policy: From Kennedy to Reagan Westport, Conn: Praeger; Johnson, P A (1998) The Government of Money: Monetarism in Germany and the United States. U.S: Cornell University Press 1986.

[13] Arestis P. New Consensus Macroeconomics: A Critical Appraisal 2009. [http://dx.doi.org/10.1007/978-0-230-29166-9_6]

[14] Taylor J. A Historical analysis of the Monetary Policy Rules. In: Taylor J, Ed. Monetary Policy Rules London: University of Chicago Press; Epstein, G (2007) Central banks, inflation targeting and employment creation Economic and Labour Market Papers. Geneve: International Labour Organization 1999. [http://dx.doi.org/10.7208/chicago/9780226791265.001.0001]

CHAPTER 5

Growth and Economic Cycles

Abstract: This chapter explores the foundations of some theories about economic growth and business cycles by surveying influential works of political economy. Firstly, we examine Adam Smith's contribution to the study of the impacts of the division and the specialization of labour on productivity and economic growth in the context of free markets. Then, we present the contribution of Joseph Schumpeter to the capitalist development based on cyclical innovations as structural changes in a long-term process of creative destruction. Finally, we consider the more recent writings of Hyman Minsky that examined the real-world of financial institutions and studied issues connected with growth, business cycles and financial institutions.

Keywords: Labour productivity, Innovative entrepreneurs, Financial fragility.

5. INTRODUCTION

This chapter is structured around great debates that have shaped our understanding of economic growth and business cycles in capitalist societies over the past 300 years. The role of free markets, technology, entrepreneurship and finance on growth and business cycles are included. We explore the foundations of some theories of economic growth and business cycles by surveying influential works of political economy.

First, we examine the classical contribution of Adam Smith that reveal an optimistic vision of the future of the free-market system because of its dynamism founded on the division and specialization of labour.

Secondly, we present the contribution of Joseph Schumpeter that privilege the cyclical study of the capitalist development. In his approach, cyclical innovations are considered structural changes that emerge in the capitalist process of creative destruction.

Finally, we consider the more recent writings of Hyman Minsky whose critical analysis focused on mainstream economics. From the Keynesian tradition, Minsky examined the real- world financial institutions and studied those problems connected with growth, business cycles and financial dynamics. Indeed, he

Maria Alejandra Madi

predicted a deep transformation of the economy after financial deregulation.

5.1. Adam Smith on Economic Progress

5.1.1. Setting the Scene

In the late 1770s, Adam Smith's early systemic contribution to political economy appeared in his book *An Inquiry into the Nature and Causes of the Wealth of Nations* (1776). At his time, the approach to the roots of economic growth was overwhelmed by the idea that the wealth of nations resulted from the accumulation of gold and silver.

Smith rejects this idea and proposed that the wealth of a nation should be measured by the total amount of its production and the total amount of commerce. In his vision of economic progress, he considers the fundamental forces that propelled the dynamics of a free market system based on individual self-interest towards increasing productivity and highly beneficial consequences to the whole society.

According to Smith, self- interest permeates all human activity and stimulates the members of a particular society to develop activities for which others are willing to pay. He believes that each human being, while searching for the fulfilling of his particular interests, turns out to contribute to the well-being of the society where he lives. In the market system, each individual - motivated by self-interest - freely chooses a trade or selects a particular task. Selfish motivations turn out to be tempered by interaction (competition) and result in social harmony.

In the late 1770s, Smith highlights the social benefits of free-market economies since the division and specialization of labour would lead to high increases in productivity. His famous description of the pin factory with ten workers shows that if each worker is specialized in a single task, the total output per worker increases at the end of the day. However, the total output per worker would decrease if each worker is involved in many tasks f the manufacture of pins.

Considering the dynamics of the free markets, Smith addresses that prices and quantities of goods to be produced are determined by competition. As Smith shows in the well-known example when people demand more gloves than shoes, i) the price of the gloves will rise as the quantity of gloves demanded exceeds the quantity supplied, ii) the price of the shoes will decrease because the quantity of shoes supplied exceeds the quantity demanded. As profits in the production of gloves become larger than usual, new producers will be stimulated to enter the market until the forces of market competition reduce the level of profit. In other words, on behalf of the higher profits, new firms start producing gloves and attract workers because of higher wages. As a result, i) the glove production rises above demand and the glove prices decrease, ii) the production of shoes falls below demand and the shoe prices increase. This price increase turns out to stimulate further shoe production. In truth, according to Smith, the balance of the markets results from the interaction of forces, such as the self-interest of workers and the competition between firms. Indeed, the self-regulating market (laissez faire) can operate without government controls to achieve economic well-being.

In the book *The Wealth of Nations*, Smith explains that by accumulating profits, capitalists can expand their business and contribute to increase national income and wealth. As the capitalists add more machines to the production process, they enhance the division and specialization of labour and increasing productivity. If the additional machinery demands more workers, this fact leads to higher nominal wages that turn out to reduce the level of profits. Indeed, this law of population addresses that as capital accumulation increases the nominal wages for workers, the amount of people in the working class will rise and finally this will push the nominal wages down. Consequently, in the long-run, profits will increase again and the capital accumulation process will continue.

After the publication of Smith's ideas, the emergence of the doctrine of *laissez-faire* did not happen soon [1]. It was not until the nineteenth century that Great Britain completed abandoned the Mercantilist agenda.

Box 25. A biographical note.

Adam Smith was born in the year of 1723, in the city of Kirkcaldy, Scotland. He studied at Burgh School and, when he was 17 years old, he went to Oxford on a scholarship and there he remained for six years.
In the year 1748, he started working as a public lecturer at the University of Edinburgh, where he met the Scottish philosopher David Hume who influenced his academic career. Some years later, Smith was offered the Chair of Logic and Chair of Moral Philosophy at the Glasgow University Faculty (1751).
In the late 1750s, after publishing *The Theory of Moral Sentiments*, Smith travelled to France as tutor of the future Duke of Buccleuch (1763–1766).
I was in the year of 1776 that Smith published *The Wealth of Nations* and one year later e was named rector of the University of Glasgow.
Adam Smith died in 1780, at the age of 67 [2].

Box 26. Selected works.

Books
1759. The Theory of Moral Sentiments
1762-63. Lectures on Rhetoric and Belles Lettres
1763. Lectures on Justice, Police, Revenue and Arms
1776. An Inquiry into the Nature and Causes of the Wealth of Nations
Collected writings and correspondence
1812. The Works of Adam Smith. With an Account of his Life and Writings
1976-1983. The Glasgow Edition of the Works and Correspondence of Adam Smith

5.1.2. Key Concepts

When reading Adam Smith, you must remember that:

1. Between the 15th and the 18th century, the expansion of commercial capitalism was characterized by geographic discoveries. Those who defended the Mercantilist agenda proposed the accumulation of gold and silver, a favourable balance of trade through increasing exports, expansion of foreign markets for English manufactured goods, high tariffs to protect the domestic industry, expansion of foreign trade to provide raw materials and a strong merchant marine. At the time of Smith, the English government extensively controlled foreign trade, prices and wages.
2. The transition from the agricultural and commercial economy to a modern industrialized economy characterized the First Industrial Revolution. In this setting, the process of enclosure forced off their land thousands of tenant farmers that became free workers and, after 1750, the steam power applied to manufacture enhanced industrial expansion.
3. The age of Enlightenment was a period overwhelmed by the faith in human reason. The doctrine of the *laissez-faire*, a product of the Enlightenment, proposed the expansion of free markets and the end of the control of the government on foreign trade.
4. In this setting, Smith highlights the role of the division and specialization of labour on productivity and market growth and proposes that the wealth of a nation should be measured by the total amount of its production and the total amount of commerce.

5.1.3. Reading Passages: The Wealth of Nations

The Reading Passages presented below were written by Adam Smith and were published in the book *An Inquiry into the Nature and Causes of the Wealth of Nations,* Book I, Chapters 1 and 2, 1776 [3]. In order to have in-depth understanding of Smith's contribution, we elaborated a summary of the main ideas.

Reading Passages	***Summary of the Main Ideas***
The greatest improvement in the productive powers of labour, and the greater part of the skill, dexterity, and judgment with which it is anywhere directed, or applied, seem to have been the effects of the division of labour.	*The division of labour improves the powers of labour directed to the production of goods.*
The division of labour, however, so far as it can be introduced, occasions, in every art, a proportionable increase of the productive powers of labour.	*The outcome of the division of labour is always the increase of labour productivity applied to producing goods.*

Contd.....

Reading Passages	Summary of the Main Ideas
The advantage is due to three circumstances (...); first, to the increase of dexterity in every particular workman; secondly, to the saving of the time which is commonly lost in passing from one species of work to another; and lastly, to the invention of a great number of machines which facilitate and abridge labour, and enable one man to do the work of many.	*The advantage of the division of labour is due to three circumstances 1) improved dexterity (2) saving of time, and (3) application of machinery,*
It is the great multiplication of the productions of all the different arts, in consequence of the division of labour, which occasions, in a well-governed society, that universal opulence which extends itself to the lowest ranks of the people.	*The wealth of a nation results from the effects of the division of labour on increasing productivity and production.*
This division of labour, from which so many advantages derived, is not originally the effect of any human wisdom, which foresees and intends that general opulence to which it gives occasion. It is the necessary, though very slow and gradual, consequence of a certain propensity in human nature which has in view no such extensive utility; the propensity to truck, barter, and exchange one thing for another.	*The division of labour emerges from the human propensity to truck, barter and exchange one thing for another.*

5.1.4. Modern Concerns About Division of Labour and Knowledge Work

Controversies about progress and labour productivity in capitalist societies have been lively in economics since Adam Smith. Recent global economic problems have only intensified the debate. Today, one issue at stake in these debates is the effects of the so-called *knowledge work*, characteristic of post-Fordism, on labour productivity, employment and working conditions.

In the context of knowledge work, companies hire multi-skills workers to develop multi-tasks within flat hierarchical structures where new innovative and decentralized practices foster new forms of employment and team work. As a result, the new trends in working conditions reveal further specialization and virtualization.

Considering a relevant feature of the virtualization of work, crowdsourcing refers to a broad pool of freelancers rapidly available in a web open call to do the necessary on–demand tasks. The employers have developed measures to evaluate the efficiency of this crowd of informal workers whose unprotected jobs in the crowdsourcing platforms are paid low wages [4]. For instance, on Amazon Mechanical Turk, workers receive up to $75/hour [5].

The new practices of crowdsourcing have been also referred to as the virtualization of the work. Indeed, technological innovations have deeply changed the labour market dynamics since homework and telework have enhanced alternative employment, working conditions and payment schemes.

Teleconferencing, video calls, instant messages and the use of social media have fostered the expansion of virtual teams of workers. Although for some workers, the virtualization of jobs could stimulate a better balance between working hours and family care, many teleworkers could not cope with the ability to fix a clear division between private life and the commitments of the virtual jobs.

Despite these deep changes in the global labour markets, even today most statistics and theories refer to typical jobs in a factory setting. Indeed, the new trends in the division and specialization of labour require a new conceptualization of employment and unemployment in the context of the digital economy.

5.1.5. Further Reading

1. Butler, E. (2007). *Adam Smith – a Primer*, The Institute of Economic Affairs.
2. Rosenberg, N. (1960). Some Institutional Aspects of the Wealth of Nations. *Journal of Political Economy,* 68 (6), 557-570.
3. Skinner, A.S., & Wilson, T. (Eds.) (1975). *Essays on Adam Smith*. Oxford: Clarendon Press.
4. Campbell, R. H., & Skinner, A.S. (1982). Adam Smith, London: Croom Helm.
5. Fleischacker, S. (2004). *On Adam Smith's Wealth of Nations: a Philosophical Companion*. Princeton: Princeton University Press.
6. Griswold, C. (1999). *Adam Smith and the Virtues of Enlightenment*. Cambridge: Cambridge University Press.
7. Raphael, D. D. (2007). *The Impartial Spectator: Adam Smith's Moral Philosophy*. Oxford: Oxford University Press.

5.2. Joseph Schumpeter on Entrepreneurship and Innovations

5.2.1. Setting the Scene

Joseph A. Schumpeter's contributions to economic theory highlights the capitalist development as a process of creative destruction. In his understanding, the cyclical process of capitalist development results from cyclical innovations that provoke qualitative and disruptive structural changes in economic and social life.

In his book *The Theory of Economic Development: An Inquiry into Profits, Capital and The Business Cycle* (1934), Schumpeter presents the circular flow and the business cycles as part of the capitalist economic evolution. The circular flow considers the static conditions of reproduction of the capitalist economy under the Walrasian general equilibrium. In the circular flow, the economic activities are founded on routine conditions that express rational decisions guided by the rule of continuity about what and how to produce. In this setting: i) firms combine the existing factors (land and labour) in accordance to their productivity;

ii) the money's functions are mainly unity of account to set prices and means of exchange of all the general interdependent individual transactions; iii) growth refers to incremental and imperceptible changes in the economic outcomes per unit of time.

By contrast to the circular flow's features, Schumpeter shows that economic development is associated with structural change in a cyclical process where qualitative transformations are highlighted. This fact results from the emergence of entrepreneurs that enhance clusters of innovations. Indeed, the process of innovation is a key-concept to the understanding of the discontinuous nature of structural change that breaks the routine of the circular flow.

In this framework, the analysis of development is connected with the concepts of entrepreneur, cyclical clusters of innovations and credit. The Schumpeterian entrepreneur differs from the rational economic agent of the circular flow as routine activities of the firms' managers are not understood as the target of entrepreneurship. However, the Schumpeterian entrepreneur is the one who introduces new products or processes in the markets by new combinations of ideas, factors of production, inputs and technological resources, for instance. In the business cycle, the qualitative and structural economic changes result from clusters of innovative investments with deep linkage effects in the economy. In this setting, the expansion of credit a driver of further competition between entrepreneurs. In Schumpetr's view, a banker is a capitalist *par excellence* that finances innovative investments by means of the creation of purchasing power of money (credit).

The cyclical process of development corresponds to a process creative destruction. The first cyclical expansion begins with the investments and outcomes of the cluster of innovations (primary wave). Old firms and industries turned out to suffer losses and to decline the level of sales due to reductions in their products' demand. During the expansion, the new entrepreneurs expand their business on behalf of the emergence of imitators with optimistic profit expectations. The multiplier effects of spending on aggregate income and induced investments (accelerating effects) characterize the underlying mechanisms of the economic expansion.

A second wave of expansion is related to unproductive credit and clusters of errors in investment decisions that result from an unfounded extreme optimism of the new entrants. At the end of the cyclical expansion, the period of recession is associated with the end of profits on behalf of intense competition. As a result of the exhaustion of the innovative period, the economic system returns to the stationary state and its functioning shows the features of a circular flow.

Box 27. A biographical note.

Joseph Alois Schumpeter was born in 1883, Triesch, Moravia. He was educated in Vienna, Austria. He studied Law at the University of Vienna and participated in the seminars presented by Eugene von Böhm- Bawerk. There he joined Ludwig von Mises, Otto Bauer and Rudolf Hilferding. In 1906, he received his doctorate and, later on, he served as the Austrian Minister of Finance for 7 months during 1909. Schumpeter wrote important economic studies and he also taught at the Universities of Czernowitz, Graz, Bonn and Harvard. At Harvard, he spent the last two decades of his life. Schumpeter died in 1950 in, Taconic, Connecticut, United States [6].

Box 28. Selected works.

Articles 1928. The Instability of Capitalism 1935. The Analysis of Economic Change *Books* 1934. The Theory Of Economic Development: An Inquiry Into Profits, Capital And The Business Cycle 1939. Business Cycles: A Theoretical, Historical and Statistical Analysis of the Capitalist Process 1943. Capitalism, socialism, and democracy 1951. Imperialism and Social Classes 1954. History of Economic Analysis

5.2.2. Key Concepts

When reading Joseph Schumpeter, you must remember that:

1. The outcomes of the cyclical cluster of innovations are qualitative and structural changes in the capitalist markets and industries.
2. The emergence of the innovative entrepreneur is associated with new social and economic facts. Indeed, the entrepreneur does not belong to the economic and social background that characterized the features of the circular flow.
3. Profits turn out to emerge with innovations. Transitory monopoly prices and profits are related to those innovative firms that expand their activities throughout the discontinuous development process.
4. Bank credit expansion means the creation of money *ex nihilo*. Bank credit is the main source of fund required by innovative entrepreneurs.

5.2.3. Reading Passages: The Analysis of Economic Change

The Reading Passages presented below were written by Joseph Schumpeter and were published in the article *The Analysis of Economic Change,* 1935 [7]. In order to have in-depth understanding of Schumpeter's contribution, we elaborated a summary of the main ideas.

Reading Passages	*Summary of the Main Ideas*
(..) practically every economic fluctuations must be historic individual and cannot be amenable to explanation but by minute historical analysis of the innumerable factors actually at work in each case. In other words, in order to understand business cycles we must first of all acquire what we termed historical experience of the way in which economic life reacts to such disturbances.	*A more realistic approach to economic fluctuations is based on the existence of many kinds of cycles rolling on simultaneously.*
(..) we shall disregard not only wars, revolutions, natural catastrophes, institutional changes, but also changes in commercial policy, in banking and currency legislation and habits of payment, variation of crops as far as due to weather conditions or diseases, changes in good production as far as due to chances discoveries, and so on. These we shall call outside factors. It will be seen that in some cases it is not easy to distinguish them from features of business behavior.	*Economic fluctuations that depend on exogenous factors are not relevant. The theoretical interest relies on the study of endogenous fluctuations.*
General equilibrium exists if every household and every firm in the domain under research is individually in a state of equilibrium in the sense of Léon Walras. It is only this last concept that matters for us.	*General equilibrium is a methodological approach adopted in the study of the circular flow.*
Obviously the face of the earth would look very different if people, besides having their economic life changed by natural events and changing it themselves by extra-economic action, had done nothing else except multiply and save. If it looks as it does, this is just as obviously due to the unremitting efforts of people to improve according to their lights upon their productive and commercial methods, *i.e.* to the changes in technique of production, the conquest of the new markets, the insertion of new commodities, and so on. This historical and irreversible change in the way of doing things we call "innovation" and we define: innovations are changes in production function which cannot be decomposed into infinitesimal steps.	*The historical and irreversible structural change happens on behalf of innovations in industrial and commercial life.*
As soon as the various kinds of social resistance to something that is fundamentally new and untried have been overcome, it is much easier not only to do the same thing again but also to do similar things in different directions, so that a first success will always produce a cluster. ..This is indeed the method of competitive capitalism which has not yet died out in trustified capitalism, to spread an improvement and to reap the social harvest- in the succeeding depression.	*Competition spread the process of innovations. However, this process does not last forever.*
(…) the waves of prosperity always do arise whenever a neighborhood of equilibrium is reached "from bellow" and (that) they always do taper off into a new neighborhood of equilibrium.	*After a wave of prosperity, the capitalist system comes back to the stationary state of the circular flow.*

5.2.4. Modern Concerns About Entrepreneurship and Innovations

Schumpeter's contribution to the apprehension of the role of innovative entrepreneurs in the development process has influenced the policy agenda of many developed and developing countries that aim to enhance technological innovation among small business, mainly start-ups. For instance, in the aftermath of the global crisis of 2007-2008, although industrial and financial policies have mainly favoured larger companies, many attempts to enhance robust and innovative entrepreneurship programs have been frustrated.

As a result, entrepreneurship sustainability has been threatened, particularly in developing countries. So far, the main obstacles to the sustainability of small firms in developing countries are: i) high tax burden, ii) little investment in technological resources, iii) insufficiency of capital and lack of credit access, iv) ignorance of the market, v) ineffective management, vi) interdependence between the private and business affairs, vii) lack of standardization and integration with trading partners, viii) difficulty to access foreign markets, ix) absence of control in processes and results, x) not specialized workers; xi) competition pressures from informal markets [8].

In truth, the concept of entrepreneurship sustainability is anchored in a Schumpeterian approach to entrepreneurship and embodied in complex learning processes and dynamic financial and technological networks that drive economic cyclical growth and development.

Currently, it is world known the relevant role of entrepreneurship in economic growth and job expansion. However, recent economic policies in developing countries do not seem to have been able to shape a sustainable entrepreneurship environment. Indeed, the particular features of entrepreneurship reveal the importance of public policies that could coordinate financial resources and stimuli for innovation (investments, processes and products). As a consequence, the promotion of entrepreneurs requires the support towards systematic innovation in products, processes and markets.

Taking into account the relevance of shaping innovation policies to enhance entrepreneurship, it is worth remembering that, in contemporary times, technological innovations are transforming business strategies and practices.

The technological impacts on the future of the economies and societies have been examined in depth by Jeremy Rifkin. His book *The Third Industrial Revolution, How Lateral Power is Transforming Energy, the Economy, and the World* (2011) underlines that we are living in the context of the Third Industrial Revolution and the TIR infrastructure—the Internet of Things—in economic and social life. The TIR platforms and connections feed Big Data to businesses, homes and vehicles in real time. Indeed, the convergence of internet technology and renewable energy is the foundation will challenge the foundations of hierarchical power and enhance later power in business and society [9].

However, this high-tech convergence deeply affects the employment and working conditions since robotics and other technologies are eliminating jobs in industrial activities, commerce and financial services, agribusiness, public services and transportation. In addition, a polarization between technological skilled and non-skilled workers could be a challenge for increasing equity in global labour markets.

5.2.5. Further Reading

1. Andersen, E.S. (2009). *Schumpeter's evolutionary economics: a theoretical, historical and statistical analysis of the engine of capitalism*. Anthem: London.
2. Andersen, E.S. (2011). *Joseph A. Schumpeter: a theory of social and economic Evolution*. Basingstoke and New York: Palgrave Macmillan.
3. Becker, M., Knudsen, T., & Swedberg, R. (Eds.) (2011). *The Entrepreneur Classic Texts by Joseph A. Schumpeter*. Standford: Standford University Press.
4. Carayannis, E. G., & Ziemnowicz, C. (Eds.) (2007). *Rediscovering Schumpeter. Creative Destruction Evolving in 'Mode 3'*. Basingstoke: Palgrave Macmillan.
5. Groenewegen, P. (2003). *Classics and Moderns in Economics: Essays on Nineteenth and Twentieth Century Economic Thought,* vol. 2, London: Routledge.
6. Harris, S. E. (Ed.) (1951). *Schumpeter: Social Scientist*. Cambridge, M A: Harvard University Press.
7. McCraw, T. K. (2007). *Prophet of Innovation: Joseph Schumpeter and Creative Destruction*. Cambridge, MA: Harvard University Press.

5.3. Hyman Minsky on Financial Instability and Business Cycles

5.3.1. Setting the Scene

In the late 1950s, Hyman P. Minsky wrote his first economic studies about the unstable dynamics of the capitalist system. He clearly shows the outstanding role of investment and the transformations of banking and central banking at the second half of the 20th century. Indeed, the real world of financial intermediaries and the problems connected with the business cycles and the functioning of the financial system are considered in his theoretical approach.

Under an institutional approach, Minsky points out how the organization of economic and social institutions helps to define policy goals and outcomes. In fact, after World War II, the nation states' economic and social agenda was oriented to growth and employment goals. In this setting, the ability of nation states to shape policy and stabilize the economy affected decentralized market processes, enhancing employment and income distribution. After financial deregulation, Minsky states that the institutional setup turned out to be inadequate to "stabilize instability". In other words, he emphasized the lost power of nation states to define long-run growth goals in a context of increasing capital mobility.

In the book *Stabilizing an Unstable Economy* (1986), Minsky rejects the neoclassical hypothesis of efficient financial markets in favour of the financial instability hypothesis [10]. Considering the non-neutral role of finance through the business cycle, he emphasizes that financial instability relies on endogenous-driven fluctuations of credit and money supply. Under this approach, in a monetary economy, credit relations, speculation and uncertainty are decisive to affect the investment path, leading to endogenous credit crunches. Indeed, the financial instability hypothesis addresses that the outcomes of financial and investment decisions should be apprehended in a changing historical framework where there are tensions and conflicts between regulators and innovative profit-seeking banks. Financial innovations impact upon banks' assets, liabilities, and capital. As a result, they provoke sudden changes in market dynamics and financial stability. He funds his contribution e contributions of John Maynard Keynes, Joseph Schumpeter and Michal Kalecki.

According to Minsky, these issues have long been ignored in the market paradigm of neoclassical economics. From the mainstream perspective, the financial crises are the result of wrong economic policy options. As a consequence, this paradigm does not consider the non-neutral role of money and financial institutions. Under the neoclassical approach, financial market imperfections might be avoided and, eventually, corrected, since adequate monetary and financial policies would be implemented. According to the hypothesis of efficient financial markets, those markets efficaciously transfer funds among economic agents.

Both empirical and theoretical aspects found Minsky's contribution that considers the dynamics of capitalist economies with complex and sophisticated financial systems. What Minsky adds to our understanding of economic instability is that banks influence the evolution of spending. Throughout the business expansion, increasing investment demand likewise puts pressure on demand for finance and funding. In this setting, the supply of short-term finance is dependent on the bankers' expectations about the performance of future profits and aggregate income. During the expansion, entrepreneurs borrow from banks and accumulate debts. Some firms speculate because of the over-optimistic perspective in their short-term returns. Minsky referred to such economic agents as "Ponzi financial units" because their income flows fall short of their debt repayment plans.

At the end of the expansion, the increase in the speculative demand for money or in the demand for other financial assets on behalf of the uncertain future, turns out to reduce the demand for capital assets. Higher liquidity preference provokes a collapse in the price of capital assets and leads to a fall in investment, profits and income. When profits and asset prices begin to decline, the credit crunch also restricts external financing for those transactions. The management of the crisis might include Central Banks' interventions as lender of last resort. Besides, this management could involve actions by the Big Government through higher spending so as to give support to private profits, preventing depression. Minsky warned that the decisive question related to the policy making process is *"Who will benefit?"* The management of financial crises might reveal the public support to private profits and the socialization of losses.

Mainly concerned about the challenges to prevent deep depressions, Minsky emphasizes the relevance of institutional reforms to manage the level of economic growth. Consequently, he presents a thorough economic proposal to prevent deep depressions. His reform agenda stimulates a reflection on the role of institutions and mainly on how the Big Government and the Big Bank (Central Bank) could simultaneously promote: a) distributional and macroeconomic effects by means of taxation; b) an employment strategy based on the creation of jobs by the government; c) a reform in financial practices biased by regulatory authorities to favour hedge financing; d) an industrial policy that would search for alternatives to the market power of giant corporations.

Box 29. A biographical note.

Hyman P. Minsky was born in 1919, Chicago, U.S. He studied mathematics at the University of Chicago (1941) and got his Ph.D. in Economics (1954) from Harvard.
Afterwards, he taught at Carnegie Tech (Carnegie Mellon University), Brown University and University of California. It was here that he developed his major monetary and financial theories.
From 1965 until his retirement in 1990, Minsky worked at Washington University in St. Louis. Since 1990 until 1996, year of his death, he was named a Levy Institute distinguished scholar and established two research programs in this institution: i) Monetary Policy and Financial Structure, and ii) The State of the U.S. and World Economies.
In 1996 he received the Veblen-Commons Award from the Association for Evolutionary Economics because of his accomplishments in academic and in public service [11].

Since 2007, interest in his work has increased because of the relevance of his analysis to the understanding of the meltdown of the U.S. mortgage-backed securities market. Firms, investors and banks tend to underestimate financial risks after a prolonged steady period of prosperity. As a consequence, further investment decisions increase the demand for finance and funding. When the market conditions change – lower sales, increase in interest rates, more restrictive credit conditions or fall in asset prices- firms and investors that are over-indebted run to liquidity. However, the lack of liquidity characterizes the so called "Minsky moment". The inability to access to new loans results from banks' restrictions on lending based on expectation of decreasing economic activity (and profits and wages) and increasing indebtedness. Speculation and financial fragility of firms and investors overwhelms the reversion of the business cycle.

Box 30. Selected works.

Working Papers and Articles
1976. A Theory of Systemic Fragility
1980. Money, Financial Markets, and the Coherence of a Market Economy
1991. Financial crises: systemic or idiosyncratic
1992. The Financial Instability Hypothesis
1993. On the non-neutrality of money
1996. Uncertainty and the Institutional Structure of Capitalist Economies
Books
1975 John Maynard Keynes
1982 Can "It" Happen Again? Essays on Instability and Finance
1986. Stabilizing an Unstable Economy.

5.3.2. Key Concepts

When reading Hyman Minsky, you must remember that:

1. The Wall Street paradigm is based on the existence of a monetary economy where investment decisions are influenced by financial institutions, speculation and uncertainty.
2. In a monetary economy, the relations between income-producing firms, financial institutions and central banks influence the valuation of the stock of capital assets, the evolution of credit and the pace of investment.
3. The portfolio structure of firms can be:
    a. **Hedge units**: firms can pay back debts and cover the interest and principal of the debt from current cash flows.
    b. **Speculative units:** current cash flows payback the amount of interest, but the firm must frequently get new credit flows to pay back the amount of the principal.
    c. **Ponzi units**: the current cash flow of firms is not sufficient to cover the interest or principal due.
4. The financial fragility hypothesis emphasizes the active role of central banks and financial institutions in shaping the cyclical path of growth in contemporary economies.

5.3.3. Reading Passages: The Financial Instability Hypothesis

The Reading Passages presented below were written by Hyman Minsky and were published in the Working Paper *The Financial Instability Hypothesis,* 1992 [12]. In order to have in-depth understanding of Minsky's contribution, we include a summary of the main ideas.

Reading Passages	***Summary of the Main Ideas***
Thus, in a capitalist economy the past, the present, and the future are linked not only by capital assets and labour force characteristics but also by financial relations.	*Capital assets, labour and financial relations connect the past, present and future of the capitalist economy.*
Expectations of business profits determine both the flow of financing contracts to business and the market price of existing financing contracts. Profit realizations determine whether the commitments in financial contracts are fulfilled--whether financial assets perform as the pro forma indicated by the negotiations	*There is a decisive connection between expectations of business profits and the evolution of financial contracts that affects the stability of* ***the capitalist system.***
The financial instability hypothesis, therefore, is a theory of the impact of debt on system behavior and also incorporates the manner in which debt is validated.	*The financial instability hypothesis is a theory that considers the outcomes of debt-income throughout the business cycle.*
Three distinct income-debt relations for economic units, which are labelled as hedge, speculative, and Ponzi finance, can be identified.	*Hedge, speculative and Ponzi finance depend on the evolution of debt –income relations through the business cycles.*
The first theorem of the financial instability hypothesis is that the economy has financing regimes under which it is stable, and financing regimes in which it is unstable. The second theorem of the financial instability hypothesis is that over periods of prolonged prosperity, the economy transits from financial relations that make for a stable system to financial relations that make for an unstable system.	*The institutional features of the financial regime of a capitalist economy are relevant to explain the instability of the economic system.*
The financial instability hypothesis is a model of a capitalist economy which does not rely upon exogenous shocks to generate business cycles of varying severity. The hypothesis holds that business cycles of history are compounded out of (i) the internal dynamics of capitalist economies, and (ii) the system of interventions and regulations that are designed to keep the economy operating within reasonable bounds.	*Business cycles are endogenous to the capitalist system.*

5.3.4. Modern Concerns About Financialization and Growth

The process of market deregulation emerged in the 1970s and, since them has fostered financial innovations that require higher leverage and risk-taking. In this setting, global liquidity, stimulated by the evolution of the American monetary policy since the early 1990s, has favoured the expansion of private capital flows and deepened the interconnections between national financial systems. As a result, global financial integration has augmented the possibilities of destabilizing the evolution of the levels of spending, output, income and employment all around the world. Hence, current economic and social challenges are not independent of global financial cycles.

In the last forty years, most governments around the world have supported the long-run process of financial expansion that turned out to be characterized as the financialization of the capitalist economy. Despite particular features of the national growth patterns, the global finance-led accumulation regime has presented some distinctive features [13]. A redefinition of the role of the state has justified privatization and deregulation in product, labour and financial markets. Changes in macroeconomic policies have turned out to focus on inflationary targets instead of employment goals. Besides, further deep structural changes have involved increasing capital mobility and the growing importance of institutional investors as managers of "financial savings". Indeed, the financialization of the global economy has produced great transformations in the growth dynamics since the decisions related to investment, production and employment are increasingly subordinated to the short-term profits.

The centralization of capital, trough waves of M&A and the expansion of sub-contracting schemes (outsourcing), has nurtured short-term profits. In fact, one of the most important changes in investment decisions resulted from the increased pressure of shareholders on the managers' performance. As a result, firm assets and investments are managed to achieve short-term profits.

Indeed, as Minsky warned, the accomplishment of profit targets involve financial innovations aimed to promote the firms' growth with lower capital requirements. Considering this background, the redefinition of employment and working conditions has been at the centre of increasing inequality. The deterioration of income distribution put downward pressures on the levels of consumption. However, on behalf of financial liberalization, households could expand the levels of consumption because they have access to credit, not only to mortgages but also to consumer loans, such as credit cards and overdraft bank accounts. Consequently, households' consumption has become increasingly dependent on banks' credit strategies and central bank's monetary policy.

As a matter of fact, monopoly-finance capital has become increasingly dependent on bubbles that, both in credit and capital markets, proved to be global sources of endogenous financial fragility. Financial and currency crises have also revealed that monetary and supervisory authorities do not cope with the complexity of the global, profit-seeking, innovative and speculative portfolios of investors and banks.

The 2007-2008 financial crisis showed sources of endogenous fragility associated with the narrow interconnections between credit and capital markets. While the price of mortgages declined, housing prices increased steadily between 1991 and 2005, lending requirements were weakened and banks managed capital requirements by expanding the securitization of loans. In other words, the credit expansion encouraged speculative decisions about assets that mainly depended on their future prices and the renewals of lending operations.

Although the capital guidelines included in the Basel II capital accord represented an improvement in terms of prudential banking regulation, the lesson learned from the crisis is that bank capital requirements are not sufficient to sustain banks' stability. In spite of greater risk-sensitivity and comprehensive coverage of risks, concerns about the weaknesses of the regulatory framework have arisen [14].

In the aftermath of the crisis, banks increased write-downs on loans while credit losses put pressure on profitability. Risk and leverage reduction strategies have been implemented to adjust capital levels to the legal requirements. Mainly in the American and European financial systems, the reduction in the volume of assets under management, lower risk-weighted assets and higher capital ratios represent a challenge for increasing profitability.

In response to the crisis, supervisory authorities have looked for setting new rules that could make the financial system more resilient according to regulatory changes [15]. Among other issues, supervisory authorities consider that

- Banks should need to hold larger capital requirements against further potential losses;
- The approval of financial products should involve extensive disclosure requirements;
- Banks should be induced to negotiate standardized products;
- Part of the credit risk should be retained on the banks' books.

The 2007-2008 global crisis showed that innovations in banks' asset-liability management have reinforced individual and systemic risks [16]. In this conjuncture, the potential threaten of financial collapse could certainly deepen unemployment and lead to a depression. Public policies turned out to subordinated to global financial and trade private strategies, instead of mainly facing social needs. Indeed, the challenges of economic growth also reveal the social and political struggles that have arisen from the dynamics of global capital reproduction in the context of financialization.

5.3.5. Further Reading

1. Cristini, A., Fazzari, S., Greenberg, E., & Leoni, R. (2015). *Cycles, Growth and the Great Recession*. London: Routledge.
2. Dyminsky, G., & Pollin, R. (2016). *New Perspectives in Monetary Macroeconomics: Explorations in the Tradition of Hyman Minsky*, Ann Arbor: The University of Michigan Press.
3. Fadda,, S., & Tridico, P. (2013). *Financial Crisis, Labour Markets and Institutions*. UK: Routledge.
4. Fazzari, S., & Papadimitriou, D. B. (Eds.) (1992). *Financial condition and macroeconomic performance: Essays in honour of Hyman P. Minsky*, London: Sharpe.
5. Kregel. J. (2014). *Economic Development and Financial Instability: Selected Essays* London and New York: Anthem Press.
6. Tavasci, D.,& Toporowski, J. (Eds.) (2010). *Minsky, Crisis and Development*. UK: Palgrave Macmillan
7. Wray, L.R. (2009). Money Manager Capitalism and the Global Financial Crisis. *Working Paper* No. 578, New York: The Levy Economics Institute of Bard College.

5.4. Policy Tools: Measures of Product Sustainability and Green Accounting

In the late 1980s, the World Commission on Environment and Development addressed that to achieve sustainable development current generations should meet their present needs without preventing future generations from meeting their own needs. More recently, the Organization for Economic Cooperation and Development defined sustainable development as the one that supports a long-term and global balance between the economy, the environment and society [17].

In the last decades, climate change and environmental disasters have revealed the need to rethink measures of product sustainability that refer to indicators, audits, indexes and accounting, as well as other reporting systems. In this setting, green accounting has emphasized the relevance of adopting new social, economic and legal standards related to environmental preservation [18].

The development of environmental accounting or green accounting became stronger in the late 1990s. The early discussions dated from the 1970s and, since the beginning, multilateral institutions, such as the United Nations, OECD and World Bank, have been actively participating in the discussions about green accounting.

In the mid-2000s, the revised version of the System of Environmental and Economic Accounts (SEEA) fostered the standardization of methodologies to guide national and international institutions in the process of getting the necessary information for adopting green accounting (Table **1**).

Table 1. Green Accounting: key developments (2000- 2009).

Year	Key Developments
2000	Publication of the manual *Integrated Environmental and Economic Accounting* by United Nations Statistics Division (UNSD) and the United Nations Envnemnt Program in order to provide guide new practices in policy making.
2003	Release of a revised version of the SEEA (System of Environmental- Economic Accounting)-1993 with progress towards the standardization of concepts, definitions and methodologies.
2004	Release of the first publication in a series of handbooks in support of the SEEA: *The Handbook of National Accounting: Integrated Environmental and Economic Accounting for Fisheries (SEEAF)* by the UNSD and the Food and Agricultural Organization.
2005	Establishment of the United Nations Committee of Experts on Environmental-Economic Accounting (UNCEEA) to promote environmental-economic accounting and related statistics standards, in conjunction with the implementation of the SEEA.
2007	The UN Statistical Commission adopted Part I of the System of Environmental-Economic Accounting for Water (SEEAW) as a temporary standard to be implemented.
2007	The UN began working on SEEA-Energy.
2008	Work related to the System of Environmental-Economic Accounting for Material Flow Accounts (SEEA-MFA) is on progress.
2009	Release of the reports on the Global Assessment of Water Statistics and Accounts and Energy Accounts by the UNSD.

Source: Adapted from Cardoso (2013) [19].

Indeed, climate change has been an important driver to develop new reporting systems and measures of economic growth. Since natural resources are public goods, green accounting has a decisive role in the interaction between companies and society. Up to now, green accounting reports have been largely voluntary. Green accounting's indicators aim to measure the environmental impacts in a period of time. If business practices provoke environmental degradation, they increase environmental *liabilities*. Indeed, the measurement of these environmental liabilities has not been easy. In many cases, the understanding of the scope of these obligations has been too subjective. More recently, those companies that voluntarily adopted green accounting methodologies have been mainly concerned with the reporting of internal environmental costs.

Environmental costs are related to the production process and are expenses that refer to the inputs oriented specifically to the preservation of the environment. There are internal environmental costs (costs supported by companies) and external environmental costs (costs supported by society). Internal costs are composed of direct or indirect, contingent or intangible environmental costs. External costs include environmental damages.

Examples of external environmental costs include, for instance: depletion of natural resources, noise and aesthetic impacts, residual air and water emissions, long-term waste disposal, uncompensated health effects, changes in quality of life. Internal environmental direct or indirect costs include, for instance: waste management, remediation costs or obligations, compliance costs, permit fees, environmental training, environmentally driven research & development, environmentally related maintenance, legal costs and fines, environmental assurance bonds, environmental certification/labelling, natural resource inputs, record keeping and reporting. Among examples of contingent costs, it is worth highlighting the impacts of: the uncertain future on compensation costs, regulatory changes, customer's demands [20].

Green accounting should be included as a quantitative basis for the management of sustainability in the set of long-term public policies oriented to economic growth. As a result, new metrics used for the measurement of sustainability - environmental, social and economic, should be formulated across countries and included to reshape the path of economic growth.

REFERENCES

[1] Allen RC. The British Industrial Revolution in Historical Perspective. Cambridge: Cambridge University Press 2009. [http://dx.doi.org/10.1017/CBO9780511816680]

[2] Heilbroner RL. The worldly philosophers: the lives, times, and ideas of the great economic thinkers 1999. Retrieved from: http://starbooksfeaa.weebly.com/uploads/5/4/8/6/54869709/the_wordly_philosophers.pdf

[3] Smith A. An Inquiry into the Nature and Causes of the Wealth of Nations 1776. Retrieved from: http://www.ifaarchive.com/pdf/smith_-_an_inquiry_into_the_nature_and_causes_of_the_wealth_of_nations%5B1%5D.pdf [http://dx.doi.org/10.1093/oseo/instance.00043218]

[4] Ipeirotis P. 2012. The (Unofficial) NIST Definition of Crowdsourcing. Retrieved from: http://www.behind-the-enemy-lines.com/search?q=cloudmechanical-turk-demographics.html; Ouye, J. (2011). Five Trends That Are Dramatically Changing Work and the Workplace. Retrieved from: http://www.knoll.com/research/downloads/WP_FiveTrends.pdf; Howe, J. (2006). The Rise of Crowdsourcing. Wired, 14 (6). Retrieved from: http://www.wired.com/wired/archive/14.06/crowds.html.

[5] Madi MA. 2015. Rethinking the labour markets: the challenges of crowdsourcing, Retrieve from: https://weapedagogy.wordpress.com/2015/11/05/rethinking-the-labour-markets-the-challen-es-of-crowdsourcing/.

[6] Swedberg R. Schumpeter: a biography. Princeton, NJ: Princeton University Press 1991

[7] Schumpeter JA. The Analysis of Economic Change. Rev Econ Stat 1935; XVII: 2-10. [http://dx.doi.org/10.2307/1927845]

[8] Madi MA. Global Finance and Business Sustainability in Brazil. Journal of Reviews on Global Economics 2013; 2: 215-22.

[9] Rifkin J. The Third Industrial Revolution, How Lateral Power is Transforming Energy, the Economy, and the World. London: Palgrave MacMillan 2011.

[10] Madi MA. Global Finance and Development India: Sanbun Publishers; Toporowsky, J (2005) Theories of Financial Disturbance. UK: Edward Elgar 2014.

[11] Levy Economics Institute of Bard College. Hyman Minsky Distinguished Scholar 2017. Retrieved from: http://www.levyinstitute.org/about/minsky/

[12] Minsky HP. The Financial Instability Hypothesis 1992. Retrieved from: http://www.levyinstitute.org/pubs/wp74.pdf

[13] Stockhammer E. Some Stylized Facts on the Finance-dominated Accumulation Regime. Compet Change 2008; 12(2): 184-202.

[14] Basel Committee On Banking Supervision (BCBS). *Overview of The New Basel Capital Accord*, Basel: BIS.; Altman, E., & Saunders, A. (2001). An analysis and critique of the BIS proposal on capital adequacy and ratings. J Bank Finance 2001; 25(1): 25-46.
[http://dx.doi.org/10.1016/S0378-4266(00)00116-3]

[15] Bank of International Settlement (BIS). Post-crisis evolution of the banking sector, Annual Report 2012. Retrieved from: http://www.bis.org/publ/arpdf/ar2012e6.pdf

[16] Saunders A, Cornett MM. Financial Institutions Management: A Risk Management Approach Columbus: McGraw-Hill College; Dermine, J,& Bissada, Y (2007) Asset and Liability Management: The Banker's Guide to Value Creation and Risk Control. London, New York: FT & Prentice Hal 2002.

[17] OCDE. Sustainable Development 2011. Retrieved from: http://www.oecd.org/greengrowth/47445613.pdf World Bank (2012). Inclusive Green Growth: The Pathway to Sustainable Development. Retrieved from: https://issuu.com/world.bank.publications/docs/9780821395516/1?e=1107022/2969166.

[18] Accounting For Sustainability. Future proofed decision making: Integrating environmental and social factors into strategy, finance and operations 2012. Retrieved from: http://www.accountingforsustainability.org/wp-content/uploads/2011/10/ A4S-Report-Future-proofed-decision-making.pdf; Grenham, T. (2010). Green accounting: a conceptual framework, Int. J. of Green Economics, 4 (4), 333 – 345.; Japan. Ministry of Environment (2005). Environmental Accounting Guidelines. Retrieved from: http://www.env.go.jp/en/policy/ssee/eag05.pdf; Yakhou, M., & Dorweilwe, V. (2004). Environmental accounting: an essential component of business strategy. Business Strategy and the Environment, 13, 65–77.

[19] Cardoso R. Green accounting. 2013. Setting the scene. In G. Chichilnisky, Ye Fah, M. A. Madi, M. Gale De Oliveira & M. Kennet (Eds.) The Greening of Global Finance. UK: The Green Economics Institute.

[20] Gale RJ, Stokoe PK. Environmental Cost Accounting and Business Strategy: Handbook of Environmentally Conscious Manufacturing. U.S.: Springer 2001.
[http://dx.doi.org/10.1007/978-1-4615-1727-6_6]

CHAPTER 6

Economic Policy

Abstract: This chapter focuses on the writings of David Ricardo, John Maynard Keynes and Friedrich von Hayek - economists whose contributions to the economic policy debate have been outstanding in real-world economics. Firstly, we present the proposal of David Ricardo, who addresses, in the 19th century, that international free trade could be beneficial for all countries. Then, we present Hayek's theoretical contribution to economic policy reinforced the free market fundamentalism over government interventions. Finally, we include Robert Mundell's contribution to the study of macroeconomic policy challenges in open economies which clearly predicted the outcomes of the transformations in exchange rate regimes and global financial regulation after the 1970s.

Keywords: Free trade, Free market fundamentalism, Open economies.

6. INTRODUCTION

Controversies around the best way to organize the economic activity—through government, through free markets or some combination of the two have always been present in the economic debates. This chapter focuses on the writings of David Ricardo, Friedrich von Hayek and Robert Mundele- economists whose contributions to the economic policy debate have been outstanding in real-world economics.

First, we present the ideas of David Ricardo, who convinced the contemporary political economists that the importance of this proposition about the benefits of international free trade. Indeed, the economic debate between those who defend government interventionists and those who privilege free markets has been also alive in the 20th and 21st centuries.

Second, we highlight the contribution of Hayek as an adversary of Keynes. The outcomes of the Great Depression fostered a deep economic discussion about full employment and government policies where Keynes was a prominent figure. In this setting, he proposed government interventions that, through the management of monetary and fiscal policies, could stimulate economic growth. However, Hayek rejected the possibility of policy management of economies and societies

Maria Alejandra Madi

and his criticism of central planning reinforces market fundamentalism. In the 1980s, his ideas were rediscovered. Indeed, the Thatcher and Reagan revolution against the interventionist welfare state revealed the victory of the free market fundamentalism over government interventions.

Finally, we consider Robert Mundell's approach to the study of macroeconomic policy challenges in open economies that clearly predicted the outcomes of the transformations in exchange rate regimes and global financial regulation after the 1970s.

6.1. David Ricardo on Free Trade

6.1.1. Setting the Scene

David Ricardo became well-known because of his contribution to the Bullion controversy in the early 1810s. On one side, the Bullionists, including Ricardo, argued that inflation results from the issue of excess banknotes and was deleterious to the interests of the English economy and society. On the other side, the Anti-Bullionists addressed that the quantity of money supply and bank notes was driven by the needs of trade. Indeed, Ricardo defended the principles of the gold standard and, therefore, he addressed that bank notes should be convertible into gold ingots.

Later on, in his *Essay on the Influence of a Low Price of Corn on the Profits of Stock* (1815), Ricardo investigated the impact of the capital accumulation process on the rate of profit and formulated the law of diminishing marginal returns. This economic law assesses that the additions to output will tend to diminish when increases in the amount of variable resources were combined in production with a fixed resource.

Ricardo also opposed to the adoption of restrictive trade policies (such as the Corn Laws) and defended deep changes in foreign trade. At this respect, he formulated the idea of comparative costs in order to show that free trade gains result from specialization and trade of different goods that countries produce at lower comparative costs.

In the year of 1817, David Ricardo published the book *Principles of Political Economy and Taxation* where he developed a theory of value in the context of a theory of distribution. In his theoretical approach, the principles of differentiation, specialization in production and perfect competition lead to an interpretation of the international market where flows of trade are based on the equilibrium of relative prices in the markets of good and services. Thus, the idea of relative prices is crucial to build international trade relations because relative prices express the competitive advantages between countries in the international setting. These ideas have been dominant in theoretical approaches to international trade for a long time.

In Chapter VII of the *Principles*, he presents a well-known example that considers: i) two countries that produce cloth and wine, ii) the labour costs are the most relevant in the analysis, iii) the productivity of labour (quantity of output produced per worker) differ across sectors of economic activity in those countries.

In his numeric demonstration, Ricardo shows that the specialization in the production of any good in each country is based on the countries' comparative advantage in production that results from a comparison between production costs of goods across countries. Ricardo's model demonstrates that free international trade is beneficial for both countries

Box 31. A biographical note.

David Ricardo belonged to a Jewish family and was born in the city of London, England, in 1772. When he was fourteen years old, he began working at the London Stock Exchange with his father. Seven years later, his family disinherited him for marrying a Quaker. Later on, he established himself in the financial market as a dealer and made a fortune.
In his late twenties, the *Wealth of Nations* (1776) stimulated Ricardo's interest in economics and later on he started writing on economic ideas for newspaper articles. After retiring from business in 1814, Ricardo decided to invest in landed estates and became a member of the British parliament and served in the period between 1819 and 1823. He actively participated in the discussion of England's economic policy issues. Ricardo died in 1823, Gatcombe Park, Gloucestershire [1].

Box 32. Selected works.

Books, papers and correspondence
The Works and Correspondence of David Ricardo
Vol. 1. Principles of Political Economy and Taxation
Vol. 2. Notes on Malthus
Vol. 3. Pamphlets and Papers 1809–1811
Vol. 4. Pamphlets and Papers 1815–1823
Vol. 5. Speeches and Evidence
Vol. 6. Letters 1810–1815
Vol. 7. Letters 1816–1818
Vol. 8 Letters 1819 – June 1821
Vol. 9 Letters 1821–1823

6.1.2. Key Concepts

When reading David Ricardo, you must remember that:

1. Free trade, as a normative aspect of the theory, is a principle that allows the

market exchanges of goods between countries to be guided by the specialization in production.

2. In the context of free trade, the exchange of goods between countries results from the differences in production costs.
3. In the context of international free trade, being the labour costs associated with the production of wine lower in Portugal than the labour costs in England for the same end, Portugal presents a comparative advantage for wine production and England for cloth production.
4. Free trade is mutually beneficial for all countries engaged in foreign trade and capital mobility equalizes the rate of profits between countries.

6.1.3. Reading Passages: On Foreign Trade

The Reading Passages presented below were written by David Ricardo and were published in the book *Principles of Political Economy,* Chapter VII, 1817 [2]. In order to have in-depth understanding of Ricardo's contribution, we elaborated a summary of the main ideas.

Reading Passages	***Summary of the Main Ideas***
Under a system of perfectly free commerce, each country naturally devotes its capital and labour to such employments as are most beneficial to each. This pursuit of individual advantage is admirably connected with the universal good of the whole.	*Capital and labour are employed in the most beneficial way under a perfect free trade system.*
England may be so circumstanced, that to produce the cloth may require the labour of 100 men for one year; and if she attempted to make the wine, it might require the labour of 120 men for the same time. England would therefore find it her interest to import wine, and to purchase it by the exportation of cloth.	*In the absence of free trade, England must devote a part of capital to the production of wine at inferior quality and quantity when compared to the wine England could buy abroad.*
To produce the wine in Portugal, might require only the labour of 80 men for one year, and to produce the cloth in the same country, might require the labour of 90 men for the same time. It would therefore be advantageous for her to export wine in exchange for cloth. This exchange might even take place, notwithstanding that the commodity imported by Portugal could be produced there with less labour than in England. Though she could make the cloth with the labour of 90 men, she would import it from a country where it required the labour of 100 men to produce it, because it would be advantageous to her rather to employ her capital in the production of wine, for which she would obtain more cloth from England, than she could produce by diverting a portion of her capital from the cultivation of vines to the manufacture of cloth.	*In the absence of free trade, Portugal would need more workers per year than England to produce cloth. On behalf of free trade, Portugal would benefit from exporting wine in exchange of cloth.*

Contd.....

Reading Passages	*Summary of the Main Ideas*
Thus England would give the produce of the labour of 100 men, for the produce of the labour of 80. Such an exchange could not take place between the individuals of the same country. The labour of 100 Englishmen cannot be given for that of 80 Englishmen, but the produce of the labour of 100 Englishmen may be given for the produce of the labour of 80 Portuguese, 60 Russians, or 120 East Indians. The difference in this respect, between a single country and many, is easily accounted for, by considering the difficulty with which capital moves from one country to another, to seek a more profitable employment, and the activity with which it invariably passes from one province to another in the same country.□	*In the absence of free- trade, England would need more workers per year than Portugal to produce wine. On behalf of free trade, England would benefit from exporting cloth in exchange of wine.*
It would undoubtedly be advantageous to the capitalists of England, and to the consumers in both countries, that under such circumstances, the wine and the cloth should both be made in Portugal, and therefore that the capital and labour of England employed in making cloth, should be removed to Portugal for that purpose	*Capitalists and consumers of England would benefit from free trade.*
(…) if capital freely flowed towards those countries where it could be most profitably employed, there could be no difference in the rate of profit, and no other difference in the real or labour price of commodities, than the additional quantity of labour required to convey them to the various markets where they were to be sold.	*In the context of capital mobility, the rate of profit between countries would equalize.*

6.1.4. Modern Concerns About the New Mercantilism

Most theories about international trade address the impact of the exchange rates on the types of specialization among countries. Traditional theories have emphasized the comparative advantages and the endowment of the primary factors of the countries, such as the Ricardian model and the Hecksher-Ohlin-Samuelson model.

The neoclassical theory of the international trade, initiated by Hecksher and Ohlin, adapted the Ricardian ideas to a model of multiple factors of production within a production function subject to constant returns (homogeneous of degree one) and perfect competition. In this mode, they also emphasized that the dynamic of international trade, that is to say, the flows of goods, is centred on the evolution of the relative prices towards the equilibrium in atomized international markets. The differences relative to the production costs, as well as the endowment of factors, are relevant: countries whose endowment of factors was more favourable in labour will have a lower labour cost and they will be specialized, consequently, in labour-intensive activities. Thus, the key-actor is the nation-state and the idea of complementary factors of productions between nations is based on comparative advantages. Under this approach, it is particularly the endowment of the factors of production mainly explains the specialization in international trade [3].

The Heckshen Ohlin-Samuelson model predicts a strong relationship between a country's abundant factor (labour or capital) and the relative prices of the goods produced. Considering

- Two countries (and their respective abundant factor): *A* (capital) and *B* (labour);
- Two goods: good *X* is capital intensive and good *Y* is labour intensive;

if the relative prices of both goods, this relation follows:

$$\frac{Px\ A}{Py\ A} < \frac{Px\ B}{Py\ B}$$

Then, country *A* would present comparative advantages in producing *X* in a free trade setting. Country *B* would produce *Y* and import *X* on behalf of its abundant factor (labour) regardless the evolution of demand.

Another criterion to evaluate the trade relations across countries is the technological content and the aggregate value of their exports, as well as the productive linkages that exporting activities create in the domestic economy. After the 1970s, new international trade models adopted the hypothesis of imperfect competition to examine how transnational corporations and intra-firms trade practices are able to influence international trade flows.

In the current global trade setting, competition and investment trends are currently driven by technological innovations that are labour-saving. According to the 2015 Information Technology and Innovation Foundation annual report, the list of "innovation mercantilist" policies includes:

- **Canada** continued to undermine pharmaceutical patents.
- **China** expanded the mandatory requirements for local data storage and included semiconductors in the industrial policy.
- **India** included mandatory local content requirements in telecom and solar power projects.
- **Indonesia and Nigeria** required mandatory local content for smart phones and obliged local data storage.
- **Russia** included mandatory local data storage and domestic production of pharmaceuticals and medical devices.
- **Turkey** protected smart phone manufacturing by adopting safeguard protection measures [4].

Throughout 2016, many countries turned to adopt protectionist policies aim at both replacing imports with domestic production of high-tech goods and services or promoting exports. In this setting, innovation mercantilist policies are being oriented to high-value technological activities and sectors, such as renewable energy, electronics, and information technology services. There are new "beggar-thy-neighbour" strategies adopted by nation-states, such as enforcement strategies to relocate productive strategies, to increase local data-storage, and to transfer technological rights.

In this respect, the 2016 Information Technology and Innovation Foundation annual report shows that:

- **China** introduced a new cyber security law and imposed (i) mandatory requirements of local data-storage, (ii) source code disclosures, and (iii) new cloud-computing restrictions.
- **Germany** enlarged the mandatory requirements of local data-storage.
- **Indonesia** introduced a patent law amendment to force local production and technology transfers along with new forced requirements of local data-storage.
- **Russia** introduced (i) mandatory requirements of local data-storage, (ii) encryption-key disclosure, (iii) restrictions to purchase foreign software.
- **Turkey** made local data-storage mandatory.
- **Vietnam** introduced mandatory requirements of local data-storage for Internet content providers along with the forced disclosure of encryption keys and source codes [5].

New protectionist trends have also been observed in the United States. At the beginning of 2017, the new American president Donald Trump's decided to remove the U.S. from the Trans-Pacific Partnership, or T.P.P. This decision signalizes that the United States are not willing to be permanently tied to East Asia, mainly a rising China, by free trade strategies. Instead, it is believed that this decision would protect American jobs in manufacturing that have diminished as a result of unfair competitive strategies followed by low-wage countries, such as Indonesia, Vietnam and Malaysia that are parties to the Trans-Pacific Partnership [6].

As America looks inward to increase investment in manufacturing, to reduce the dependence on East Asia imports and to stimulate job creation, among other domestic challenges, the outcomes of the revision of free trade policies will certainly carry out relevant geopolitical implications.

6.1.5. Further Reading

1. Blaug, M. (1958). *Ricardian Economics: A Historical Study*. New Haven: Yale University Press, 1958.
2. Chang, H. (2002). *Kicking Away the Ladder: How the Economic and*

Intellectual Histories of Capitalism Have Been Re-Written to Justify Neo-Liberal Capitalism. London: Anthem Press.
3. Hollander, S. (1979). *The Economics of David Ricardo*. Toronto, Ontario: University of Toronto Press.
4. Irwin, D. A. (1998). *Against the Tide: An Intellectual History of Free Trade*. Princeton, NJ: Princeton University Press.
5. Milgate, M., & Stimson, S.C. (1991). *Ricardian Politics*. Princeton, NJ: Princeton University Press.
6. Milgate, M., & Stimson, S.C. (2009). *After Adam Smith: A Century of Transformation in Politics and Political Economy*. Princeton, NJ: Princeton University Press.
7. Napoleoni, C. (1976). *Smith, Ricardo, Marx: Observations on the History of Economic Thought*. New York: Halsted Press.
8. Schonhardt-Bailey, C. (2006). *From Corn Laws to Free Trade: Interests, Ideas, and Institutions in Historical Perspective*. Cambridge, MA. The MIT Press.

6.2. Friedrich Hayek on the Role of the Government

6.2.1. Setting the Scene

Friedrich von Hayek's contribution to monetary theory and economic policy has been overwhelmed by a broad discussion about the scope and effects of government interventions in the competitive economic order. As a defender of the competitive order, he highlighted that only the price market system can solve the fundamental problem in economics that is the coordination of independent individual's plans and decisions.

In the 1930s, Hayek's theoretical approach privileges the analysis of the impacts of government interventions, through changes in monetary policy, on investment decisions and industrial fluctuations. After a period of credit expansion stimulated by expansionary monetary policy, the decisions of consumers and entrepreneurs will be influenced by the evolution of relative prices. Investment decisions will continue increasing till raising prices of capital goods reduce the profit rate towards its equalization to the lower level of the interest rate.

Critical to the utilization of the monetary policy as a stimulus to economic growth, Hayek addressed that this stimulus induce inefficiency in long-term capital allocation because of the artificial interest rates managed by central banks. After the War World II, he expanded the criticism of Keynes's proposals of aggregate demand management to promote economic growth and reduce unemployment through expansionary monetary and fiscal policies. In truth, he definitely rejected the anti-cyclical spending agenda.

Although Hayek believed that the promotion of price stability and high employment were not necessarily in conflict, price stability should be privileged by economic policy. In his 1974 Nobel Prize Lecture, *The Pretense of Knowledge*, Hayek addressed that the Keynesian agenda will lead to macroeconomic instability and higher systemic inefficiency.

In the book *Denationalisation of Money- the Argument Refined* (1976), Hayek clearly showed discontent with the evolution of central banks' practices that turned out to accommodate the financial demands from the government bureaucratic apparatus. Consequently, these practices promoted inflationary policies through arbitrary interventions in the economic order [7].

Box 33. A biographical note.

Friedrich von Hayek was born in 1899, Vienna, Austria, and became a legal British citizen in 1938. In 1917, he served in the Austro-Hungarian Army and years later he completed his studies at the University of Vienna.
In the year of 1929, he published the book *Monetary Theory and the Trade Cycle*. In the 1930s, he gave lectures on monetary theory at the London School of Economics and Political Science (LSE) where he also took part in a debate with Keynes. He was finally selected as the Tooke Professor of Economic Science and Statistics at LSE. After leaving the LSE in the early 1950s, he became professor at the University of Chicago for almost 12 years. In 1962, he returned to Europe and worked at the University of Freiburg in Germany until his retirement in 1968.
In 1974, Hayek received the Nobel Prize in Economics along with the Swedish economist Gunnar Myrdal. During 1977, he returned to the University of Freiburg and, in the early 1980s, he started working on a book about his criticism of socialism. However, due to health problems, he couldn't finish this book project and died in 1992, in Freiburg, Germany [8].

Box 34. Selected works.

Articles and lectures
1937. Economics and Knowledge
1945.The Use of Knowledge in Society
1974. The Pretense of Knowledge
Books
1937. Individualism and Economic Order
1944. The Road to Serfdom
1960. The Constitution of Liberty
1976. Denationalisation of Money: The Argument Refined
1978. New Studies in Philosophy, Politics, Economics, and the History of Ideas
1995. Contra Keynes and Cambridge: essays, correspondence
2008. Hayek on Hayek: An Autobiographical Dialogue
Collected essays and correspondence
(1991-2015) The Collected Works of F.A. Hayek

Hayek proposed the denationalization of money to foster price stability. The privatization of money should require free monetary markets where only the stable currencies would survive. He believed that no central bank is able to gather the necessary information to many the money supply. Indeed, in Hayek's opinion, no government is able to define the path of the economy and society, or even to provide the so called public goods, since he believed that growing state interventions turns out to be, in fact, a threaten for democracy and the free society values.

The spread of the neoliberal agenda revealed the victory of Hayek's ideas about the relevance of price stability and about the deleterious outcomes of monetary and fiscal policies oriented to promote economic growth.

6.2.2. Key Concepts

When reading Friedreich von Hayek, you must remember that:

1. The coordination of multiple and independent individual plans and decisions is the fundamental problem in Economics. Only the competitive price market system can achieve such coordination.
2. Rational economic agents consider that market prices are signals that reveal relevant market information to make economic calculations.
3. No government can gather sufficient information in order to elaborate future plans for the economy and society.
4. The economic policy should privilege price stability.

6.2.3. Reading Passages: The Denationalization of Money

The Reading Passages presented below were written by Friederich von Hayek and were published in the book *Denationalisation of Money: The Argument Refined*, 1976 [9]. In order to have in-depth understanding of Hayek's contribution, we elaborated a summary of the main ideas.

Reading Passages	***Summary of the Main Ideas***
(…) all major inflations until recently been the result of governments covering their financial 'needs' by the printing press.	*Major inflations are caused by monetary expansion oriented to face the financial needs of governments.*
(…) Ministers of finance were told by economists that running a deficit was a meritorious act, and even that, so long as there were unemployed resources, extra government expenditure cost the people nothing, any effective bar to a rapid increase in government expenditure was destroyed.	*The popularity of Keynesian economics is founded on a wrong understanding of the functioning of the market economy.*

Contd.....

Reading Passages	*Summary of the Main Ideas*
If we are to preserve a functioning market economy (and with it individual freedom), nothing can be more urgent than that we dissolve the unholy marriage between monetary and fiscal policy, long clandestine but formally consecrated with the victory of 'Keynesian' economics.	*It is highly undesirable in any circumstances that funds for government spending should be provided by the creation of additional money.*
One (the process of budgetary monetary financing) which even men who genuinely wish to avoid it find it impossible to stop.	*The process of budgetary monetary financing is a self-accelerating process since this style of finance (the Keynesian style) turns out to create new expectations of further inflation.*

6.2.4. Modern Concerns About Austerity

Throughout recent decades, the interactions between central banks, financial institutions and investors have revealed the search for the enlargement of financial access to credit and capital markets.

Soon after the 2007-2008 global financial crisis, expansionary monetary policies have been adopted to stabilize the financial markets. In this setting, current sovereign debt challenges have left newly elected leaders at the mercy of foreign creditors and capital flows.

The search for macroeconomic austerity requires short-term tax increases, expenditure cuts and selling assets. However, in the long-term, austerity measures negatively affects economic growth rates and induce high employment rates in the context of structural reforms [10].

As a result, social vulnerability increases among working and retired people. Changes in employment and working conditions, besides the loss of rights, threaten the livelihoods of working people by decreasing wages. Besides, the management of pension plans that have been affected by austerity measures turns out to redefine the future of retired workers. Indeed, as a result of austerity programs, many governments have disappointed their citizens.

The maintenance of the neo-liberal agenda by means of the spread of “good governance” practices is based on the supposition that is possible to shape right 'institutions' in a competitive order.

These practices also involve reconfiguring politics to better facilitate the required changes. The neoliberal agenda, following Hayek’s suggestions, should foster the promotion of institutional reforms to guarantee that the free-market capitalist system works “appropriately”, even at the expense of increasing social inequality.

6.2.5. Further Reading

1. Buckley Jr., W.F., & Machlup, F. (Eds.) (1976). *Essays on Hayek*. NY: New York University Press.
2. Butler, E. (2012). *Friedrich Hayek: The Ideas and Influence of the Libertarian Economist*. Hampshire, Great Britain: Harriman House.
3. Caldwell, B. (2013). *Hayek's The Road to Serfdom: A Brief Introduction*. Chicago: University of Chicago Press.
4. Ebenstein, A. (2003). Hayek's Journey: The Mind of Friedrich Hayek. NY: Palgrave Macmillan.
5. Feser, E. (Ed.) (2013). *The Cambridge Companion to Hayek*. Cambridge: Cambridge University Press.
6. Miller, E. F. (2010). *Hayek's The Constitution of Liberty: An Account of Its Argument*. UK: Institute of Economic Affairs.
7. Peart, S. J., & Levy, D. M. (2013). *F. A. Hayek and the Modern Economy*. NY: Palgrave Macmillan.
8. Wapshott, N. (2011). *Keynes Hayek: The Clash That Defined Modern Economics*. New York: W. W. Norton & Company.

6.3. Robert Mundell on Capital Mobility and Exchange Rates

6.3.1. Setting the Scene

The contribution of Robert Mundell to international economics predicted the challenges for macroeconomic policies in open economies. Indeed, the adoption of floating exchange rates and high capital mobility characterize current monetary regimes in the context of globalization. However, throughout the Bretton Woods system, almost all countries adopted fixed exchange rates. At that time, capital and exchange rate controls restricted capital mobility. After the crisis of the Bretton Woods System in the early 1970s, Mundell's analysis proved to be increasingly relevant for policy-makers.

In the 1960s, he published the article *Capital Mobility and Stabilization Policy under Fixed and Flexible Exchange Rates.* After the foreign trade and capital mobility suppositions were introduced into the IS-LM model of a closed economy, the Mundell-Fleming model has been considered the macroeconomic model for open economies. Although Mundell's contribution predominates in the model, Marcus Fleming (who died in 1976) also worked at the IMF during the period of Mundell's affiliation. Both of them developed research in stabilization policies in open economies.

In Mundell's research, among other relevant questions, he addressed: How do the effects of the integration of international capital markets depend on the adoption of fixed or floating currencies? Should a country participate in a currency area?

Robert Mundell shows how the outcomes of stabilization policies in open economies depend on the degree of international capital mobility and the exchange rate regime:

- Under a floating exchange rate regime and with a high degree of international capital mobility, the management of monetary policy is efficient to achieve higher levels of aggregate income.
- Under a fixed exchange rate regime and with a high degree of international capital mobility, the management of fiscal policy is efficient to achieve higher levels of aggregate income

Newer versions of his macroeconomic model for open economic improved the dynamics approach, differentiated stock and flows and also considered the rhythm of market adjustment. In addition, they explored how prolonged imbalances in the balance of payment could arise and be eliminated. Among the conclusions, we can highlight:

- Under fixed exchange rates and low degree of international capital mobility, an expansionary monetary policy will reduce the level of interest rates and raise the level of domestic aggregate demand. In the adjustment process, the resulting balance of payments deficit will provoke monetary outflows. These outflows in turn put pressure upward on the interest rate and downwards on the domestic aggregate demand till the balance of payments equilibrium.
- Under flexible exchange rates and high degree of international capital mobility, an expansionary monetary policy will reduce the level of interest rates and will also raise the level of domestic aggregate demand. In the adjustment process, the resulting balance of payments deficit will provoke monetary outflows that put pressure on the exchange market and promote the devaluation of the currency. As a result, exports are stimulated and the domestic aggregate demand increases till the balance of payments equilibrium.

Box 35. A biographical note.

Robert A. Mundell was born in Canada in 1932. In the 1950s, after studying Economics at the University of British Columbia in Vancouver, he developed graduated courses at the University of Washington (Seattle) and at the Massachusetts Institute of Technology. At that time, Paul Samuelson and Charles Kindleberger influenced his studies, as well as Lionel Robbins and James Meade. In 1956, h finished his doctorate thesis on international capital movements that was supervised by James Meade. Mundell taught at the University of British Columbia, Stanford University, Johns Hopkins Bologna Center of Advanced International Studies and University of Chicago. After attending conferences all over Europe, he was invited by the European Community to formulate alternative plans for currency unification, in 1969.
He left the University of Waterloo in 1971 and has been affiliated to Columbia University (New York) since 1974. In the late 1990s, he co-founded the Zagreb Journal of Economics and, two years later, he received the Nobel Memorial Prize in Economic Sciences for his contribution to the study of economic policy under different monetary arrangements and of optimum currency areas [11].

Box 36. Selected works.

Articles and lectures
1961. A Theory of Optimum Currency Areas
1963. Capital Mobility and Stabilization Policy under Fixed and Flexible Exchange Rates
1968. The Collapse of the Gold Exchange Standard
1997. The International Monetary System in the 21st Century: Could Gold Make a Comeback?
1999. A Reconsideration of the Twentieth Century.
Books
1968. International Economics
1968. Man and Economics
1977. The New International Monetary System
1985. Macropolicies in the World Economy and the New Capitalist Revolution
1997. The International Monetary System in the 21st Century: Could Gold Make a Comeback?

Taking into consideration the increasing degree of international capital mobility, Mundell considers the role and challenges of "optimum currency areas". Among the advantages, lower transaction costs in foreign trade and less uncertainty in the expectations about relative prices can be included. Among the drawbacks, there are challenges to face asymmetric shocks and to orient the policy to full employment without reductions in real wages. In an optimum currency area, the only high labour mobility would ensure full employment after asymmetric shocks.

6.3.2. Key Concepts

When reading Robert Mundell, you must remember that in open economies:

1. The volatility of fixed exchange rates managed by central banks has been a concern in the context of increasingly higher international capital mobility.
2. In the context of a fixed exchange rate regime and high international capital mobility, the management of fiscal policy can increase the levels of aggregate income.
3. A floating exchange rate is determined by the interaction of supply and demand in the exchange market.
4. Under floating exchange rates and high international capital mobility, the management of monetary policy is efficient to increase the levels of aggregate demand.

6.3.3. Reading Passages: A Reconsideration of the Twentieth Century

The Reading Passages presented below were written by Robert A. Mundell and were published in the Nobel Prize Lecture *A Reconsideration of the Twentieth Century,* 1999 [12]. In order to have in-depth understanding of Mundell's contribution, we elaborated a summary of the main ideas.

Reading Passages	*Summary of the Main Ideas*
The century can be divided into three distinct, almost equal parts. The first part, 1900-33, is the story of the international gold standard, its breakdown during the war, mismanaged restoration in the 1920's and its demise in the early 1930's. The second part, 1934-71, starts with the devaluation of the dollar and the establishment of the $35 gold price and ends when the United States took the dollar off gold. The third part of the century, 1972-1999, starts with the collapse into flexible exchange rates and continues with the subsequent outbreak of massive inflation and stagnation in the 1970's, the blossoming of supply-side economics in the 1980's, and the return to monetary stability and the birth of the euro in the 1990's. The century ends, however, with our monetary system in deficit compared to the first decade of the century and that suggests unfinished business for the decades ahead.	*The whole 20th century can be divided into three parts bon behalf of different international monetary arrangements.*
The international gold standard at the beginning of the 20th century operated smoothly to facilitate trade, payments and capital movements. Balance of payments were kept in equilibrium at fixed exchange rates by an adjustment mechanism that had a high degree of automaticity. The world price level may have been subject to long-terms trends but annual inflation or deflation rates were low, tended to cancel out, and preserve the value of money in the long- run. The system gave the world a high degree of monetary integration and stability.	*The first part of the 20th century, from its beginning to the 1930 Great Depression, was characterized by operation of the international gold standard with fixed exchange rates and high degree of monetary integration.*
In the new arrangements, which were ratified at Bretton Woods in 1944, countries were required to establish parities fixed in gold and maintain fixed exchange rates to one another.	*After the Second Word War, the United States maintained an asymmetric role in the international monetary arrangement with fixed exchange rates and gold convertibility.*
In August 15, 1971, confronted by requests for conversion of dollars into gold by the United Kingdom and other countries, President Nixon took the dollar off gold, closing the “gold window” at which dollars were exchanged for gold with foreign central banks. The other countries now took their currencies off the dollar and a period of floating began.	*In the early 1970s, the international monetary arrangement moved to a floating exchange system without gold convertibility. The dollar was the most important currency.*
The introduction of the euro redraws the international monetary landscape. With the euro- upon its birth the second most important currency in the world, - a tri-polar currency world involving the dollar, euro, and yen came into being. The exchange rates among these three islands of stability will become the most important prices in the world economy.	*After 1999, the euro re-shaped the world currency system.*
The volatility of exchange rates is especially disturbing among countries each of which have achieved, according to local definitions and indexes, price stability. The volatility therefore measures real- exchange- rate changes and involves dysfunctional shifting between domestic and international-goods industries and aggravates instability in the financial markets.	*In the context of financial integration, exchange rate volatility can provoke economic disturbances.*

6.3.4. Modern Concerns About Global Governance

Robert Mundell deeply studied the interconnections between the international financial integration and the effectiveness of macroeconomic policies. He predicted the macroeconomic challenges in open economies.

Since the 1980s, multilateral institutions, such as the International Monetary Fund (IMF), have defended the adoption of financial deregulation in the economic policy agenda because of its long-term benefits in allocating global capital flows. According to the IMF, financial deregulation could promote: a) lower costs of domestic credit; b) risk diversification; c) access to new products, technologies and markets; d) higher competition between domestic and foreign players [13]. However, in the last decades, international flows of capital have not been able to support economic development. Indeed, deregulated financial markets have fostered the volatility of exchange rates and other price assets. Indeed, the financial crisis of 2007-2008 showed that financial deregulation increased the volatility of capital flows and macroeconomic instability.

In this setting, most of the discussions about capital mobility do not take into account a key-problem: the specific forms of integration in financial globalization and the international currency hierarchy [14]. Financial crises have shown sources of financial fragility of many countries on behalf of systemic problems.

Current international financial architecture is composed of institutions, practices and instruments. Most multilateral institutions were designed in the 1940's, at the time when financing the reconstruction of the post-World War II was essential. Financial deregulation was first implemented by industrialized countries after the crisis of Bretton Woods. Since the late 1960s, the U.S. government has gradually loosened restrictions on banks and, after the abolition of the Glass-Stegall Act of 1933, commercial banks have started to act as investment banks.

In the aftermath of the 2007-2008 crisis, the existing international financial architecture proved to be useless to prevent or warn about this crisis [15]. As a result, growing global concerns enhanced changes in the regime of prudential banking regulation towards Basel III. Looking back, Basel II capital accord, based on the ratio of a bank's capital to its risk-adjusted assets, shaped an institutional set up where banks' capital adequacy aimed to improve the efficiency of financial markets in the allocation of resources. This financial set-up oriented by the Bank of International Settlements' "codes and patterns" proved to enhance asset-liability management, or even, balance sheet management, to reduce legally capital requirements.

The lesson learned after the global crisis of 2007-2008 is that capital requirements are not sufficient to guarantee financial stability. As a matter of fact, the concern about the weaknesses in the regulatory framework has arisen. First, segmented supervisory authorities do not cope with the universal scope of banks. Second, new regulatory frameworks are generally proposed after banking innovations.

After the crisis, the supervisory authorities in the financial markets have been looking for setting new rules within Basel III capital accord that could make the financial system more resilient according to regulatory targets. Among other issues, the financial supervisory authorities have forced 1) larger capital requirements against further potential losses, 4) liquidity requirements and leverage constraints will also be considered. Nevertheless, lower risk-weighted assets and higher capital ratios represent threatens for financial stability.

The global crisis indicated that the structure and dynamics of current global finance, as a historical set of institutions, products, procedures, behaviours and policies potentially materialized the risk of collapse of the financial system with deep negative consequences for the real economy and society.

Indeed, we need a serious revision of the role of global governance [16]. The convergence of multiple crises – food, energy, environmental, financial, social – in combination with the rise of new global political and economic players have driven deep transformations worldwide. In the future, global coordinated actions are necessary within the main international agencies. One of the great challenges to other kind of global governance is the lack of agreement among developing countries that makes their economic difficulties even greater. So far, the possibilities of other global governance oriented to managing globalization and providing public global goods seem to be remote.

6.3.5. Further Reading

1. Obstfeld, M.,& Rogoff, K. (1996) *Foundations of International Macroeconomics*. Cambridge, Massachusetts: MIT Press.
2. DeGrauwe, P. (2000). *Economics of Monetary Union* (4th ed.). New York: Oxford University Press.
3. *Calvo, G. A., & Reinhart, C. M. (2002). Fear Of Floating,* The Quarterly Journal of
4. *Economics*, 117 (2), 379-408.
5. Fleming, M. (1978). *Essays on Economic Policy*. New York: Columbia University Press.
6. Rodriguez, C. (1979). Short- and Long-Run Effects of Monetary and Fiscal Policies Under Flexible Exchange Rates and Perfect Capital Mobility. *American Economic Review*, 69, 176–82.

7. Diaz-Alejandro, C. (1985). Good-bye Financial Repression, Hello Financial Crash. *Journal of Development Economics*, 19 (12), 1–24.

6.4. Policy tools: Targeted Interventions in Financial Products

In order to support sustainable development, it's definitely time to rethink the policy agenda about prudential regulation and supervision of systemic risk. The global financial setting has created new demands for reform and new regulation after the 2007-2008 financial crisis.

The mission of the Bank for International Settlements (BIS) located in Basel, Switzerland, is to serve central banks in their pursuit of monetary and financial stability, to foster international cooperation and to act as a bank for central banks. Created in 1930, the BIS is the oldest multilateral financial organization.

In the late 1980s, the first Capital Accord introduced capital requirements on risk-weighted assets, mainly considering credit-risk. Known as Basel capital accords, they have been voluntarily adopted to develop efficient financial systems and greater transparency to financial regulators and investors. Actually, the main idea is that more capital in itself could prevent financial crises.

However, financial regulators should also regulate product intervention instruments in the banking system. Indeed, they should be equipped to take a more proactive approach with targeted interventions. In order to reduce consumer's risks, regulators could force changes in some features of the set of financial products offered by banks [17].

The main objectives of these targeted interventions are:

1. Reduction of consumers' risks and losses favoured by the lack of understanding of labelling and terminology of retail financial products;
2. Limitation or avoidance of the need for future prescriptive regulation;
3. Improvement of the consumer confidence and trust in the financial system;
4. Improvement of the efficiency of the financial system through increased consumer engagement and participation.

In this attempt, financial regulators should intervene in the financial system to require or impose:

- Amendments to marketing and disclosure materials,
- Distribution restrictions,
- Product banning.

These interventions should be subjected to a judicial review mechanism. Besides, financial regulators could limit the interventions in relation to a product or class of products for 12 months. However, temporary interventions could be extended if more time is required by financial institutions to change relevant practices.

Indeed, this policy tool demands a proactive market-based financial regulator. To reduce consumer's risks and losses, financial regulators should also consider the creation of Financial Education programs oriented not only to warn consumers about labelling and terminology of financial products but also to address domestic budget management guidelines.

REFERENCES

[1] Library of Economics and Liberty. 2017. David Ricardo. *The Concise Enciclopedia of Economics*. Retrieved from: http://www.econlib.org/library/Enc/bios/Ricardo.html; Editors of the International Encyclopedia of the Social Sciences (2017) Ricardo, David. *International Encyclopedia of the Social Sciences*. Retrieved from: http://www.encyclopedia.com. http://www.encyclopedia.com/people/social-sciences-and-law/economics-biographies/david-ricardo.

[2] Ricardo D. Principles of Political Economy 1817. Retrieved from: http://www.econlib.org/library/Ricardo/ricP.html

[3] Madi MA, Gonçalves JR. International Economics. In: Reardon J, Ed. The Handbook of Pluralist Economics Education. London, New York: Routledge 2009.

[4] InformationTechnology and Innovation Foundation. The Worst Innovation Mercantilist Policies of 2015 Report 2016. Retrieved from: https://itif.org/publications/2016/01/11/worst-innovatio--mercantilist- policies-2015

[5] InformationTechnology and Innovation Foundation. The Worst Innovation Mercantilist Policies of 2016 Report 2016. Retrieved from: https://itif.org/publications/2017/01/09/worst-innovatio--mercantilist-policies-2016?mc_cid=f79695c248&mc_eid=42bb6a1c96. (Guillochon 1993). (Krugman and Obstfeld 2003).

[6] Bakerjan P. 2017. Trump Abandons Trans-Pacific Partnership, Obama's Signature Trade Deal. *The New York Times*. Retrieved from: https://www.nytimes.com/2017/01/23/us/politics/tpp-trump-tra-e-nafta. html?_r=0

[7] Madi MA. 2015. Dissolving the 'unholy marriage': Hayek's recommendation on monetary and fiscal policy. *Journal of Contemporary Economic And Business Issues*, 2 (2), 23-38. Retrieved from: http://www.eccf.ukim.edu.mk/Article/141

[8] Lindbeck A (Ed). 1992. Friedrich August von Hayek – Biographical. Retrieved from: https://www.nobelprize.org/nobel_prizes/economic-sciences/laureates/1974/hayek-bio.html; Kukathas, C. (2012). Friedrich Hayek and liberalism. In D. Edmonds & N. Warburton (Eds.) Philosophy Bites Back, Oxford: Oxford University Press.

[9] Hayek F. Denationalisation of Money: The Argument Refined 1976. Retrieved from: https://mises.org/sites/default/files/Denationalisation%20of%20Money%20The%20Argument%20Refined_5.pdf.

[10] Madi MA. 2015. Teaching macroeconomics: Austerity programs, citizenship and labour. Retrieved from: https://weapedagogy.wordpress.com/2015/07/15/teaching-macroeconomics-austerity-progr-ms-citizenship-and-labour.

[11] Frängsmyr T. 2000. Robert A. Mundell.Biographical. Retrieved from: http://www.nobelprize.org/nobel_prizes/economic-sciences/laureates/1999/mundell-bio.html.

[12] Mundell RA. A Reconsideration of the Twentieth Century 1997. Retrieved from: http://www.nobelprize.org/nobel_prizes/economic-sciences/laureates/1999/mundell-lecture.html.

[13] Fischer S. Capital Account Liberalization and the Role of the IMF 1997. Retrieved from: https://piie.com/fischer/pdf/Fischer141.pdf.

[14] Flassbeck J. The exchange rate: economic policy tool or market price? Discussion Papers 157. Geneve: UNCTAD 2001.

[15] Ugarteche O, Puyana A, Madi MA. 2015. The Need for a New International Financial Architecture. In O. Ugarteche, A. Puyana & M. A. Madi (Eds.) Ideas towards a new international financial architecture?. UK: WEA books.; Kregel, J. (2009). Managing the Impact of Volatility in International Capital Markets in an Uncertain World, Retrieved from http://ssrn.com/abstract=1394465 or http://dx.doi.org/10.2139/ ssrn.1394465; Marichal, C. (2010). Nueva historia de las grandes crisis financieras: una perspectiva global 1873-2008. Buenos Aires: Debate.; Ocampo, J. A. (2014). Reforming the Global Reserve System. Retrieved from http://library.fes.de/pdf-files/iez/global/10900.pdf

[16] Griffith-Jones S. 2002. Uma nova arquitetura financeira internacional como bem público global. In R. Fendt & M. A. Tedesco Lins. (Ed.) Arquitetura Assimétrica: o espaço dos países emergentes e o sistema financeiro internacional. RJ: Fundação Konrad Adenauer.; Kaul, I., Conceição, P., Le Goulven, K.,& Mendoza, R. (Eds.) (2003). Providing public global goods: managing globalization. Oxford: Oxford University Press.

[17] Banco De Portugal. 2012. Relatório de Supervisão Comportamental 2 0 1 1, Lisboa, Portugal.

CHAPTER 7

Welfare, Social Justice and Governance

Abstract: This chapter provides a range of economic and philosophical perspectives drawing from the classic writings of Arthur Pigou, Amartya Sen and Elinor Ostrom. Firstly, we present the contribution of Arthur Pigou that highlights the relevance of government interventions to address the impacts of externalities on social welfare. Then, we consider Amartya Sen's ideas that show deep concerns about justice in contemporary economic theory and public policy. Finally, we present the contribution of Elinor Ostrom to the management of common-pool resources, at local and global levels.

Keywords: Welfare, Capabilities, Governance of commons.

7. INTRODUCTION

Since the days of Adam Smith, concerns on welfare, justice and fairness have been closely intertwined in economic thought. Today, these topics are relevant to the current economic debate because Western societies are facing increasing social challenges because of unsustainable patterns of growth. Indeed, the outstanding feeling is that the outcomes of so called "progress" have been economic instability, deleterious working conditions and inequality. As a result, opinions about the threatens of globalization have increased founded on a deep criticism of the 'Washington Consensus' agenda that privileges deregulation and free markets as pillars of economic growth.

This chapter provides a range of economic and philosophical perspectives drawing from the classic writings of Arthur Pigou, Amartya Sen and Elinor Ostrom. First, we present the contribution of Arthur Pigou on externalities. The British economist highlights the relevance of government intervention to address the impacts of externalities on social welfare.

Second, we consider the ideas of Amartya Sen that put together economic theory, social choice theory and moral philosophy to develop an approach to justice. Indeed, departing from economics and philosophy, Sen highlights the role of ethics in addressing economic and social problems.

Maria Alejandra Madi

Finally, Elinor Ostrom adds to our understanding in economics how institutional arrangements, in a diverse set of ecological and social economic political settings, affect human behaviour and economic outcomes. Indeed, she highlighted the relevance of polycentric systems of governance to address a sustainable governance of the commons. As Ostrom warned, there is one ideal governance regime, but a variety of regimes of governance that may achieve sustainability. Indeed, she addressed that institutional arrangements influence the governance of urban policies, private business and natural resources.

7.1. Arthur Pigou on the Economics of Welfare

7.1.1. Setting the Scene

Arthur Cecil Pigou's economic studies and research were preceded by philosophic reflections on ethics, the nature of science and methodological issues. He further explored, as Alfred Marshall's pupil, the conditions that prevent perfect markets from guaranteeing the maximization of benefits for all society. In Pigou's understanding, the foundations of welfare are the individual's satisfactions or utilities. Individual economic welfare refers to the satisfaction or utility that an individual gets from his expenditure on goods and services. According to him, social welfare is considered as the sum of all individual welfares of society.

In the book *Wealth and Welfare* (1920), Pigou concludes that improved economic welfare would result from national income growth, income redistribution to poor people and lower income variability and, in particular, lower variability of the share of national income received by poor people. In this book, he highlights that the gap between the marginal net social product and the marginal private net product reduce the levels of welfare. Pigou also emphasizes the relevance of the concept of externalities that refer to costs or benefits not considered by economic agents that takes action in economic activities. As a result, he suggests taxes or subsidies that are now called Pigouvian taxes and subsidies.

The British economist addresses that the existence of negative or positive externalities in the markets is a sufficient justification for government intervention. If economic activities in the production of goods and services create negative externalities, such as pollution and health problems, a tax should be imposed on this activity to discourage it.

Moreover, if economic activities in production create positive externalities—for instance by enhancing higher levels of education, subsidies should be granted for those activities that create such positive externalities. In other words, when social net product diverges from private net product at the margin, a compensation mechanism can be introduced in the markets by the imposition of a tax or the creation of a subsidy.

Lionel Robbins challenged this approach to welfare economics because it is based on the supposition that utility is measurable and because it is a normative approach. Also, in the 1960s, Ronald Coase rejects the need of taxes and subsidies if those people affected by externalities and the economic agents that create them can easily get together and bargain [1]. Besides, public choice economists put in question the efficacy of the Pigouvian taxes and subsidies because governments fail just as markets do. However, up to now, most economists still consider that the Pigovian taxes are efficient policy instruments to improve welfare.

Box 37. A biographical note.

Arthur Cecil Pigou was born in Ryde, Isle of Wight, United Kingdom, in the year of 1877. He began his studies at King's College in 1896 and, three years later, he obtained a Bachelor of Arts degree. Afterwards, Pigou developed his studies on economics, ethics and political philosophy. He was largely influenced by Alfred Marshall's ideas.

After being a fellow of King's College, he worked as professor of Economics at Cambridge University. He won the Adam Smith prize at Cambridge (1903) for an essay which was published in 1905 as *Principles and Methods of Industrial Peace*. This essay was the basis for the lectures that he presented at the University College London in the period between 1903 and 1904.

His theoretical research on equilibrium economics was crucial to build the foundations for his work on welfare economics. Arthur Pigou died in 1959 [2].

Box 38. Selected works.

Articles
1904. Monopoly and Consumers' Surplus
1910. Producers' and Consumers' Surplus
1927.The Law of Diminishing and Increasing Cost
1928. An Analysis of Supply
1947. Economic Progress in a Stable Environment
Books
1912. Wealth and Welfare
1920. The Economics of Welfare
1927. Industrial fluctuations
1928. A study in public finance
1933. The Theory of Unemployment
1952. Essays in Economics

7.1.2. Key Concepts

When reading Arthur Pigou, you must remember that:

1. Social welfare is regarded as the aggregation of individual welfares. Each individual attempts to maximize the satisfaction or utility from his expenditure

on different goods and services. Different people derive the same satisfaction or utility out of the same real income. Satisfactions or utilities can be compared across people considering that the gain in utility of an additional amount of income to a poor man is greater than the loss of utility to a rich man from the same amount of income.

2. National income growth generally results social welfare improvement if it does not reduce the share of income of the poor people.
3. Any income redistribution that favours poor people without reduction in national income improves social welfare.
4. The existence of negative or positive externalities in the markets is a sufficient justification for government intervention by means of taxes or subsidies.

7.1.3. Reading Passages: The Economics of Welfare

The Reading Passages presented below were written by Arthur Pigou and were published in the book *The Economics of Welfare,* Part II, Chapters 2 and 3, 1920 [3]. In order to have in-depth understanding of Pigou's contribution, we elaborated a summary of the main ideas.

Reading Passages	***Summary of the Main Ideas***
The marginal net product of a factor of production is the difference that would be made to the aggregate product by withdrawing any (small) unit of the factor.	*The marginal product of a factor of production refers to the marginal increment of resources in any given use or place.*
(…) We have next to distinguish precisely between the two varieties of marginal net product which I have named respectively social and private.	*Divergences between social and private marginal net product arise because of the existence of positive or negative externalities, that is to say, of costs or benefits that result from private decisions.*
Again an increase in the quantity of resources employed by one firm in an industry may give rise to external economies in the industry as a whole and so lessen the real costs involved in the production by other firms of a given output.	*When the social net product is higher that marginal private net product, the presence of external economies enhances lower costs in the industry.*
(…) If private and social net products everywhere coincide, the free play of self-interest, so far as it is not hampered by ignorance, will tend to bring about such a distribution of resources among different uses and places as will raise the national dividend and, with it, the sum of economic welfare to a maximum.	*When the social net product equalizes private net product, the sum of economic welfare is maximum in free markets.*

Contd.....

Reading Passages	*Summary of the Main Ideas*
The essential point for our present purpose is that, when marginal private net products and marginal social net products coincide, any obstacles that obstruct the free play of self-interest will, in general, damage the national dividend. In real life, of course, marginal private and marginal social net products frequently do not coincide.	*Free markets do not always equalize private and social net products in all markets.*

7.1.4. Modern Concerns About Externalities and Climate Change

An important report published in 2009 by the British Sustainable Development Commission arose doubts if capitalism's propensity for efficiency will actually allow current generations to stabilize climate change outcomes and protect society against resource scarcity. Although environment challenges are a world-wide concern, too many economists continue to pay little attention to the biophysical dimensions of current business models and patterns of growth [4].

In the context of financialization, deep concerns have arisen about the outcomes of the patterns of energy and consumption because they are passing down social and environmental safeguards. In the last decades, market deregulation opened up investment opportunities in sectors where private enterprises and foreign companies were formerly subject to restrictions, such as mining, energy and telecommunications. In spite of some local resistance, market liberalization was introduced in many countries historically dominated by state-owned, vertically-integrated monopolies. As a matter of fact, the spending patterns and energy investments have been overwhelmed by tensions between governments, global investors, transnational corporations and citizens.

As Pigou warned, government market interventions are required when the private net product exceeds the social net product at the margin. In truth, there are many challenges to globally fix those externalities provoked by the outcomes of climate change. Firstly, the recent United Nations Conference of the Parties, the so called COP, has revealed that global negotiations lack coordination between governments and the private sector to articulate spending patterns and energy policies. Secondly, there is the educational challenge to introduce teaching practices and enlarge the access to information related to environmental and disaster mitigation of risks. Thirdly, there is the low-carbon investment challenges for shaping suitable public policies.

Indeed, a deep understanding of the externalities created by climate change cannot be achieved without considering how climate change touches on economic growth and welfare theories.

7.1.5. Further Reading

1. Blaug, A. (Ed.) (1992). *Arthur Pigou (1877-1959)*. Aldershot, England: Edward Elgar.
2. Coase, R. (1960). The problem of social cost, *Journal of Law and Economics*, 3, 1-44.
3. Knight, F.H. (1924). Some fallacies in the interpretation of social cost, *Quarterly Journal of Economics*, 38 (4), 582-606.
4. Meade, J. (1952). External economies and diseconomies in a competitive situation, *Economic Journal,* 62 (245), 54-67.
5. Mishan, E.J. (1971). The postwar literature on externalities: an interpretive essay, *Journal of Economic Literature,* 9 (1), 1-28.
6. Scitovsky, T. (1954). Two concepts of external economies, *Journal of Political Economy,* 62 (2), 143-151.
7. Turvey, R. (1963). On the divergence between social cost and private cost, *Economica*, 30 (119), 309-313.

7.2. Amartya Sen on Capabilities and Justice

7.2.1. Setting the Scene

Amartya Sen considers the existing conditions in the world in which we live to understand the main economic and social challenges of our times. He argues that globalization has deepened social differences and increased polarization between groups whose social, economic and cultural identity comports with Western industrial countries and groups whose behaviour is still attached to more traditional values.

Beyond income inequality, his concerns rely on health, education, unemployment, and social exclusion. Different historical legacies in the assets of human capital and institutional development shape the path to future development. Low literacy rates, poor health, weak governance and institutions, the lack of infrastructure all hinder economic and social development. In his research on human livelihoods, Sen explores how various social and economic factors do not only influence the behaviour and achievements of different groups of people in each society but also condition the actual opportunities of living.

Sen's comprehensive account of the capability approach in the book *Development as Freedom* (1999) synthesizes many of his particular contributions. The capability approach claims that well-being is to be analysed in terms of people's capabilities and take into account a plural set of features of human life [5]. To assess social disparities, the inequality of capabilities is of central relevance. Considering that freedom should play a key role in well-being, capabilities refer to the *actual opportunities* of living. Indeed, there is a contrast between capabilities and achievement. The capabilities' approach does not focus on the actual abilities to do what the person values doing. Therefore, the framework of the capability approach is not tied to achieve functionings.

Indeed, Sen emphasizes that idea of capability is oriented towards freedom and opportunities and should be considered in a broader informational perspective. When thinking in terms of communities, he states that it is necessary to consider how capabilities could be aggregated into one overall assessment of quality of life. In this attempt, the choice of the relevant set of capabilities for measuring the quality of life involves value judgments. In practical terms, groups tend to select them by using mechanisms such as deliberative participatory exercises or enduring consensus and associated legitimacy. However, the capability approach is consistent with limited agreements in values and principles.

Sen's contribution to the theory of social choice opened space towards the study of rules for collective decisions. The capability approach favours the analysis of broad and relevant information in order to shape immediate policy interventions oriented to expand human capabilities of all members of society. Departing from this background, his book *The idea of Justice* (2009) explores the foundations of a theory of justice that highlights the role of governments at the local and global levels in facing the demands for justice, such as the demands for sustainable development.

In the attempt to formulate a theory of justice that aims at the formulation of new policy strategies and interventions, Sen argues for a renewal of the bond between the two disciplines: philosophy and economics.

Box 39. A biographical note.

Amartya Sen was born in Santiniketan, India, in 1933. He got a PhD from the University of Cambridge in 1959 and has made his academic career as professor in India, the United Kingdom and the United States. Among other activities, we can highlight his contributions as President of the following organizations: the Econometric Society, the American Economic Association, the Indian Economic Association, and the International Economic Association. His awards include Bharat Ratna (India); Commandeur de la Legion d'Honneur (France); the National Humanities Medal (U.S.); Ordem do Merito Cientifico (Brazil); Honorary Companion of Honour (UK); the Aztec Eagle (Mexico); the Edinburgh Medal (UK); the George Marshall Award (U.S.); the Eisenhower Medal (U.S.); and the Nobel Prize in Economics in 1998 [6].

7.2.2. Key Concepts

When reading Amartya Sen, you must remember that:

1. Income inequality, health, education, unemployment and social exclusion should be integrated into a multifaceted analysis of well-being.
2. Capability is the aspect of freedom related to individual substantive opportunities in society.
3. The capability approach focuses on the actual ability to do different things that a person values doing.
4. Economics should be concerned with justice.

Box 40. Selected works.

Books
1982. Choice, Welfare and Measurement
1982. Poverty and Famines: An Essay on Entitlement and Deprivation
1985. Commodities and Capabilities
1987. The Standard of Living
1988. On Ethics and Economics
1992. Inequality Reexamined
1997. Resources, Values, and Development
1999. Development as Freedom.
2002. Rationality and Freedom.
2004. Capabilities, Lists, and Public Reason: Continuing the Conversation
2005. Human Rights and Capabilities
2007. Identity and Violence: The Illusion of Destiny
2009. The Idea of Justice
2010. The Place of Capability in a Theory of Justice
Articles and book chapters
1984. Well-Being, Agency and Freedom: The Dewey Lectures
1993. Capability and Well-being
1995. Gender Inequality and Theories of Justice
2010. The Place of Capability in a Theory of Justice

7.2.3. Reading Passages: The Possibility of Social Choice

The Reading Passages presented below were written by Amartya Sen and were published in his Nobel Prize Lecture *The Possibility of Social Choice,* 1998 [7]. In order to have in-depth understanding of Sen's contribution, we elaborated a summary of the main ideas.

Reading Passages	*Summary of the Main Ideas*
How are we best to determine whether a society is developing for the better or the worse? This is a question which has occupied philosophers and social scientists for centuries. In a democracy, all answers to this question must contain some rule, which enables us to aggregate the social values, held by each and every member of society into one common value - a social preference.	*In a democratic society, there must be a rule to aggregate social preferences.*

Contd.....

Reading Passages	*Summary of the Main Ideas*
Social choice theory is a very broad discipline, covering a variety of distinct questions, and it may be useful to mention a few of the problems as illustrations of its subject matter. When would a majority rule yield unambiguous and consistent decisions? How do we measure aggregate poverty in view of the various predicaments and miseries of the diverse people that make up a society? How can we accommodate rights and liberties of persons giving adequate recognition to their preferences? How do we appraise social valuations of public goods such as natural environment or epidemiological security?	*Social choice theory refers to relevant investigations about the relations between individuals and society.*
Our deeply felt, real-world concerns have to be substantively integrated with the analytical use of formal and mathematical reasoning.	*A real-world approach is a must to apprehend social challenges.*
There may indeed be a case for taking incomes, or commodity bundles, or resources more generally, to be of direct interest in judging a person's advantage, and this may be so for various reasons- not merely the mental states they may help to generate.	*Interpersonal comparisons cannot be only based on mental states.*
There is, thus, an important need to go beyond income information in poverty analysis, in particular to see poverty as capability deprivation.	*Poverty is a multi-faced concept.*

7.2.4. Modern Concerns About Gender Issues

The high degree of economic inequality has negative implications for economic growth and sustainability and also affects social cohesion and political stability. Indeed, the apprehension of current global inequality involves the understanding of the deep tensions between the outcomes of the hypertrophy of financial expansion and the expectations of society about citizenship, employment and income. In current debates about income inequality, gender issues have also been present.

At the intersection of justice, welfare and economics, gender issues have been also considered by Amartya Sen. Indeed, the capability approach is central to address the aspect of freedom related to substantive opportunities opened for women. It focuses on women's actual ability to do different things that they value doing.

In the global scenario, the women's challenges are great. First, women earn less than men, even doing the same jobs and having the same levels of formal education. Second, women spend more time on household and childcare than men. Third, women globally represent the larger percent of people that live on less than a dollar a day. Forth, women do not usually get leadership positions in business and politics. Finally, the outcomes of the 2007-2008 global financial crisis have been more intensely affecting women in formal labour markets.

Despite the ongoing initiatives of the United Nations (UN) Millenium Goals toward gender issues, the outcomes of the global financial crisis revealed the presence of labour market discrimination against women in developing countries, such as Brazil [8]. Their participation is stronger as domestic workers, besides occupations in services and trade where working hours are longer. In spite of the highest educational levels of women compared to men, the average nominal wages among women is lower than average nominal wages of men. In addition to the wage gap, women are facing increasing turnover. Precarious jobs, mainly based on short-term contracts, enhance the vulnerability of workers, mainly women with informal jobs. Indeed, women are more likely to lack decent working conditions.

In addition to these challenges in the labour market, the increasing weight of unpaid work is more likely when women become unemployed and return to their homes and take more responsibility for housework than men, or because the loss of family income makes it impossible to support the remuneration of domestic workers [9]. In this setting, the expansion of cash transfer programs in many developing countries has been decisive to reduce women's vulnerability to the economic crisis.

The understanding of this social reality is relevant to rethink public policies in order to privilege the role of gender issues in job generation and promote women empowerment. As a matter of fact, decent female work is important for improving the overall opportunities and advantages of women in current societies.

7.2.5. Further Reading

1. Agarwal, B., Humphries, J., & Robeyns, I. (Eds.) (2005). *Amartya Sen's Work and Ideas: A Gender Perspective*. New York: Routledge.
2. Alkire, S. (2002). Valuing Freedoms: Sen's Capability Approach and Poverty Reduction. Oxford: Oxford University Press.
3. Brighouse, H., & Robeyns, I. (Eds.) (2005). Measuring Justice: Primary Goods and Capabilities. Cambridge: Cambridge University Press.
4. Comin, F., Qizilbash, M., & Alkire, S. (Eds.) (2008). *The Capability Approach: Concepts, Measures and Applications*. Cambridge: Cambridge University Press.
5. Crocker, D.A. (2009). *Ethics of Global Development: Agency, Capability, and Deliberative Democracy*. Cambridge: Cambridge University Press
6. Deneulin, S., & Shahani, L. (Eds.) (2009). *An Introduction to the Human Development and Capability Approach: Freedom and Agency*. London: Earthscan.
7. Nussbaum, M. (2000). *Women and Human Development: The Capabilities*

Approach. Cambridge: Cambridge University Press.
8. Nussbaum, M. (2011). *Creating Capabilities: The Human Development Approach.* Cambridge, MA: Harvard University Press.

7.3. Elinor Ostrom on Governing the Commons

7.3.1. Setting the Scene

In her famous book, *Governing the Commons* (1990), Elinor Ostrom focuses on the capacity of people around the globe to create long-run resilient arrangements for protecting environmental resources. In particular, she studies how groups of people manage and preserve common-pool resources such as forests and water supplies. However, collective actions have not inevitably emerged in all groups of people.

Ostrom defines *common or common-pool resources* as public goods with finite benefits. Therefore, common-pool resources can be potentially used beyond the limits of sustainability because of the lack of exclusion of users. This creates an incentive for increasing the rate of use of this resource above its physical or biological renewal. Besides, *common property* is a kind of institutional arrangement about ownership and responsibility. Considering this framework, Ostrom builds a theoretical approach to the management of common-pool resources at local and global levels. There is one ideal governance regime, but a variety of regimes of governance that includes:

- Rules of appropriation of resources;
- Rules of maintenance of resources;
- Rules of monitoring and enforcement of the appropriation and obligation activities;
- Rules for of conflict resolution;
- Evaluation of the performance of the resource system and the strategies of participants to change previous rules.

The users of common-pool resource can work together to the sustainable governance of their commons by collective action [10]. Successful commons' self-governance depends on: the coherence between the resource environment and its self-government structure; the enforcement of rules through effective monitoring and sanctions; and the adoption of low-cost conflict resolution mechanisms. According to Ostrom, adaptive governance refers to changing rules and enforcement mechanisms over time since institutional arrangements are able cope with new conditions and needs.

In the late 2000s, the approach to social and ecological systems considers the complexity of natural and human systems. These complex systems enable citizens, governments, businessmen, and resource users to deal with collective-action problems at diverse scales. When applying this framework to the governance of commons in urban areas, Ostrom arrives at the following conclusions:

1. Preferences about public goods and services tend to be more homogeneous in neighbourhoods than in metropolitan areas;
2. In the context of multiple jurisdictions, citizens can more effectively articulate preferences, define problems and choice packages of urban goods and services. As a result, if necessary, they can move to other jurisdictions;
    1. Competition for contracts in urban goods and services fosters technological innovations and the search for social co-production.

In short, Elinor Ostrom adds to our understanding how polycentric arrangements of governance can influence economic outcomes, human behaviours and institutions towards sustainable collective actions. In this attempt, she crossed traditional boundaries between academic disciplines.

Box 41. A biographical note.

Elinor Olstrom was born in the year of 1933 in California, United States. After studying at Beverly Hills High School, she got a master's degree (1962) and a Ph.D. (1965) in political science from the University of California. At that time, she married Vincent Ostrom. After finishing her doctorate, she became professor in the Indiana University Department of Political Science in 1974. Over her long career, international activities included extensive field experiences in underdeveloped countries, such as in Africa, Asia and Latin America. Her research was supported by multilateral organizations, foundations and the American government. She participated in many professional associations, in particular the American Political Science Association, serving as Vice President (1975-76) and as President (1996-97). She was also president of the Public Choice Society (1982-1984), the International Association for the Study of Common Property (1990-91), and the Midwest Political Science Association (1984-1985). Member of the editorial board of 24 journals, Ostrom was awarded 12 honorary doctorates from universities. Besides, she was Founding Director of a Center for the Study of Institutional Diversity at Arizona State University in the late 2000s. In 2009, she and Oliver E. Williamson won the 2009 Nobel Prize in Economic Sciences. She was the first woman to win the Nobel Economics Prize. She died in 2012, in Bloomington, Indiana. At the time of her death, she was a Distinguished Professor of Political Science at Indiana University, senior research director of the Vincent and Elinor Ostrom Workshop in Political Theory and Policy Analysis at Indiana University (https://ostromworkshop.indiana.edu/), and founding director of the Center for the Study of Institutional Diversity at Arizona State University [11].

Box 42. Selected works.

Articles and book chapters
1985. Are successful efforts to manage common-pool resources a challenge to the theories of Garrett Hardin and Mancur Olson?
1985.The rudiments of a revised theory of the origins, survival and performance of institutions for collective action
1987. Institutional Arrangements for Resolving the Commons Dilemma: Some Contending Approaches
2007. A Diagnostic Approach for Going Beyond Panaceas
2009. A general framework for analyzing sustainability of social-ecological systems
2012. Polycentric Systems: Multilevel Governance Involving a Diversity of Organizations
Books
1990. Governing the Commons: The Evolution of Institutions for Collective Action
2010. Working together: Collective Action, the Commons, and Multiple Methods in Practice

7.3.2. Key Concepts

When reading Elinor Ostrom, you must remember that:

1. Common-pool resources are a type of public goods.
2. Common property is an institutional arrangement that regulates ownership and responsibility.
3. Social-ecological systems are complex systems that couple natural and human systems.
4. Polycentric systems of governance refer to a theoretical approach to build collective-actions.

7.3.3. Reading Passages: Beyond Markets and States

The Reading Passages presented below were written by Elinor Ostrom and were published in her Nobel Prize Lecture *Beyond Markets and States: Polycentric Governance of Complex Economic Systems,* 2009 [12]. In order to have-in-depth understanding of Ostrom's contribution, we elaborated a summary of the main ideas.

Reading Passages	***Summary of the Main Ideas***
A core effort is developing a more general theory of individual choice that recognizes the central role of trust in coping with social dilemmas. Over time, a clear set of findings from the micrositational level has emerged regarding structural factors affecting the likelihood of increased cooperation. Due to the	*To effectively cope with social dilemmas, institutional rules should fit into a specific social-ecological setting.*

Contd.....

Reading Passages	*Summary of the Main Ideas*
complexity of broader field settings, one needs to develop more configural approaches to the study of factors that enhance or detract from the emergence and robustness of self-organized efforts within multilevel, polycentric systems. Further, the application of empirical studies to the policy world leads one to stress the importance of fitting institutional rules to a specific social-ecological setting. "One-size-fits-all" policies are not effective.	
In the mid-twentieth century, the dominant scholarly effort was to try to fit the world into simple models and to criticize institutional arrangements that did not fit.	*In the 1950s, simple economic models oriented the policy making process. These models privileged dichotomies, such as: market and state, consumers and producers, private and public goods.*
The mid-twentieth-century world views of simple systems have slowly been transformed as a result of extensive empirical research and the development of a framework consistent with game-theoretical models for the analysis of a broad array of questions.	*In the second half of the 20th century, scholars have been slowly shifting to use more complex frameworks, theories, and models in order to understand the diversity of puzzles and problems in contemporary societies.*
Vincent Ostrom, Charles Tiebout, and Robert Warren (1961) introduced the concept of polycentricity in their effort to understand whether the activities of a diverse array of public and private agencies engaged in providing and producing of public services in metropolitan areas was chaotic, as charged by other scholars – or potentially a productive arrangement.	*Polycentric systems of governance refer to potential productive arrangements that deal with the provision and production of public services.*
Forests, water systems, fisheries, and the global atmosphere are all common-pool resources of immense importance for the survival of humans on this earth.	*Common- pool resources could be classified into four groups.*
The most important lesson for public policy analysis derived from the intellectual journey I have outlined here is that humans have a more complex motivational structure and more capability to solve social dilemmas than posited in earlier rational-choice theory.	*Public policy analysis should rethink the motivations and the capabilities of human beings to solve social challenges.*

7.3.4. Modern Concerns About the Commodification of Science

Through economic history, textile machines, steam-powered transport, machine tools, steel, besides electrification belonged to different phases of scientific and technological progress.

Looking back, the relations between science and society were fundamentally changed at the wartime mobilization and reconstruction. Through wartime, scientists were asked to engage in large-scale, multidisciplinary and government-funded projects that range from electronics to atomic energy.

After the 1950s, petrochemical products, automobiles, information technologies and biotechnologies, especially genetic modification, compose a scenario where science and technology seem to subordinate nature and overwhelm social life. In the aftermath of World War II, scientific research involved research councils, scientific advisory boards, expert commissions and specialized government agencies in different areas, such as health, agriculture and especially atomic energy. The target was to transform the scientific development in a commercially profitable process [13].

In the mid 1960s, deep concerns arose about the social outcomes of scientific trends. Indeed, in Western societies, the criticisms of the governance and uses of scientific resources grew. Indeed, throughout the postwar era, new kinds of chemical products have been introduced- especially fertilizers, insecticides and additives used in food production. High concern arose on behalf of health and environmental costs that resulted from the use of insecticides in agriculture.

Looking back, earlier scientific development clearly expressed different specific types of competence and knowledge. As a result, the classical categories of science and engineering have been founded on particular types of scientific and technological theories such as physical, biological, chemical, mechanical, *etc.* However, biotechnology industries, as genetic engineering, information technology, nanotechnology and synthetic biology require the contributions of a wide range of fields of research. In other words, these advanced scientific fields are founded on transdisciplinary knowledge approaches. Information technologies, biotechnologies and nanotechnologies develop a new mode of transdisciplinary research in networks or systems of innovation that have been developed by Japanese, Americans and European Union countries. In this setting, some universities have effectively sold the resulting technological products.

In recent times, the governance of science fostered the commodification of science. In Western societies, the governance of scientific resources is, in fact, growing links between scientists and the business world. This interconnection has involved new institutional arrangements, such as the restructuring of research institutions and of many scientific fields. In short, technology is spilling over into every aspect of social lives. In this context, the targets and governance of scientific resources that has been mainly adapted to face the needs and values of business [14].

As Elinor Ostrom extensively addressed, all commons are prone to challenges within the space domain on behalf of irresponsible use. Considering her contribution towards governance issues, institutional change and collective action, current generations need to rethink its engagement in the governance of common-pool resources. As Ostrom warned, there is one ideal governance regime, but a variety of regimes of governance to achieve a better governance of common-pool resources. In this attempt, scientific resources should be shared in order to provide solutions to the relevant problems that humanity faces.

7.3.5. Further Reading

1. Agrawal, A. (2007). Forests, Governance, and Sustainability: Common Property Theory and its Contributions. *International Journal of the Commons*, 1(1), 111-136.
2. Fennell, L. A. (2011). Ostrom's Law: Property Rights in the Commons. *International Journal of the Commons*, 5(1), 9-27.
3. Gibson, C. C. (2005). In pursuit of better policy outcomes. *Journal of Economic Behavior and Organization*, 57 (2), 227–230.
4. Hardin, G. (1968). *The tragedy of the commons*. Science, 162,1243–1248.
5. Ostrom, V. (1980). Artisanship and artifact. *Public Administration Review*, 40(4), 309–317.
6. Ostrom, V., Tiebout, C.M., & Warren, R. L. (1961) The organization of government in metropolitan areas: A theoretical inquiry. *American Political Science Review,* 55(4), 831–42.
7. Wagner, R. E. (2005), Self-governance, polycentrism, and federalism: recurring themes in Vincent Ostrom's scholarly oeuvre. *Journal of Economic Behavior and Organization,* 57 (2), 173–88.

7.4. Policy Tools: Small Firms and Public Policies

Actually, the apprehension of the economic features of small businesses aims to reduce their vulnerability to economic shocks [15]. Today, it is urgent to create new conventions based on a new business agenda that could cope with focus on small business growth. The new agenda should express a holistic approach to sustainable development (inequalities, poverty, global warm, *etc.*). Indeed, the business environment would not only fulfil the interests of entrepreneurs, but also benefit the society as a whole.

Changes in institutional arrangements toward business sustainability rely on rules, norms and actions that could favour inclusive growth. Thus, policy recommendations have to be tailored in order to face the needs of small firms. Actually, small firms need to access external sources of credit, knowledge and technology in order to both develop innovations and to reach new markets and new costumers. In this attempt, they should engage in networks, particularly those that share knowledge and competencies that are critical to pursue competitive strategies. Indeed, for the vast majority of small firms, the creation and reinforcement of competitive advantages should be articulated to business networks and clusters closely interrelated with public policies.

Considering that access to finance, innovation and knowledge is outstanding, public policies should be oriented to three key-issues: finance, technology and knowledge. Among the targets of public policies, we can highlight:

1) Finance

- Increase the access to credit for innovation
- Favour the reduction of interest rates and fees charged in credit operations
- Encourage the creation of cooperatives
- Increase the access to risk capital for startups
- Reduce bureaucracy and reform the tax system in order reduce the burden on small firms
- Formulate credit policies to stimulate innovations and generate decent jobs.

2) Innovation

- Create technological incubators
- Improve the law of protection of trademarks and patents for entrepreneurs
- Extend the access of technological innovations in different sectors
- Formulate market regulatory policies to protect innovative small firms

3) Knowledge

- Enhance news forms of business cooperation, networking and clustering strategies
- Enlarge technical support in order to improve management practices in small firms

Appropriate responses to the small firms' needs in finance, innovation and knowledge vary depending across countries on behalf of the institutional arrangements of governance, economic resources and cultural factors. Indeed, the "one-size-fits-all" solutions are unwarranted to promote welfare, social justice and sustainability.

REFERENCES

[1] Coase RH. The Problem of Social Cost. J Law Econ 1960; 3(1): 1-44. [http://dx.doi.org/10.1086/466560]

[2] Knight K, McLure M. 2009. The Elusive Arthur Pigou. *Discussion Paper*. Business School, University of Western Australia. Retrieved from: http://www.business.uwa.edu.au/__data/assets/pdf_file/0005/2068628/ 12-05-The-Elusive-Arthur-Pigou.pdf

[3] Pigou Ac. The Economics of Welfare 1920. Retrieved from: http://oll.libertyfund.org/titles/ pigou-th--economics-of-welfare

[4] Foster JB. A Failed System: The World Crisis of Capitalist Globalization and its Impact on China. Mon Rev 2009; 60(10): 1-23. [http://dx.doi.org/10.14452/MR-060-10-2009-03_1]

[5] Robeyns I. 2016. The Capability Approach. In: E. N. Zalta (Ed.) *The Stanford Encyclopedia of Philosophy*. Rerieved from: https://plato.stanford.edu/archives/win2016/entries/capability-approach/

[6] Biographical note 2017. Rerieved from: http://scholar.harvard.edu/sen/biocv

[7] Sen A. The possibility of Social Choice 1998. Rerieved from: http://www.nobelprize.org/nobel_prizes/economic-sciences/laureates/1998/sen-lecture.pdf

[8] United Nations. Kennet M, Felton J, Winchester A, Gale De Oliveira M, Eds. *Millenium Declaration*. New York: United Nations.; Madi, M. A. C. (2012). Women and the global crisis: access to work and inequalities in Brazil. Green economics: women's unequal pay and poverty. UK: The Green Economcis Institute 2000.

[9] Antonopoulos R, Hirway I, Eds. Unpaid Work and the Economy: Gender, Time-Use and Poverty in Developing Countries. UK: Palgrave Macmillan 2010. [http://dx.doi.org/10.1057/9780230250550]

[10] Chow T. An Introduction to Ostrom's Eight Principles for Sustainable Governance of Common-Pool Resources as a Possible Framework for Sustainable Governance of Space 2012. Rerieved from: https://swfound.org/media/61531/isusymposium2012paper_tchowbweeden.pdf

[11] Grandin K. Elinor Ostrom 2010. Biographical. Retrieved from: https://www.nobelprize.org/nobel_prizes/economic-sciences/laureates/2009/ostrom-bio.html; McCay, B. J., & Bennett, J. (2014). Elinor Ostrom 1933–2012. Biographical memoires. National Academy of Sciences. Retrieved from: http://www.nasonline. org/publications/biographical-memoirs/memoir-pdfs/ostrom-elinor.pdf

[12] Ostrom E. Beyond Markets and States: Polycentric Governance of Complex Economic Systems 2009. Retrieved from: http://www.nobelprize.org/nobel_prizes/economic-sciences/ laureates/2009/ostrom-lecture. html

[13] Jamison A. Science and Technology in Postwar Europe. In: Stone D, Ed. Oxford Handbook in Postwar European History. Oxford: Oxford University Press 2012. [http://dx.doi.org/10.1093/oxfordhb/9780199560981.013.0032]

[14] Madi MA. Commodification of science and technology 2016. Retrieved from: https://weapedagogy.wordpress.com/2016/07/29/commodification-of-science-and-technology

[15] Madi MA. Small Business in Brazil: competitive global challenges. NY: Nova Publishers 2016.

CONCLUSION

Throughout these *Pluralist Readings*, the combination of historical focus with the discussion of modern issues and debates permits to appreciate the ongoing dialogue between classical and contemporary views in Economics. Throughout this ongoing dialogue, we highlighted, among other issues:

- Alternative accounts of the development of economic thought
- Concerns about the limitations of economics as a specific discipline
- Classic debates and discussions on economic policy
- New developments within economics, both those that challenge and those that extend the economic research towards interdisciplinary approaches.
- Joint research efforts conducted by researchers from different disciplines to create new conceptual, theoretical and methodological frameworks to address current sustainability challenges.

Indeed, these *Pluralist Readings* aim to foster the awareness of diversity of ideas within Economics without aiming to classify the selected authors into the orthodox/ heterodox dichotomy that overwhelms the economic debate. The scope of the selected contributions involves broad topics in Economics and open debates about theoretical approaches and policy matters.

A BRIEF OVERVIEW

The expansion of financialization, while economic growth remains uncertain, has spread unemployment, income gaps and less welfare in the 21st century. The institutional set up that has threatened the supply of public social services and kept labour cheap turned out to favour the expansion of global corporations, financial asset portfolios and new business models. Besides, the new millennium challenges the foundations and dynamics of representative democracies because of the role of financial power over economic, social and political life.

Taking into account this background, these *Pluralist Readings* explore a pluralist intellectual path, through the historical evolution of economic ideas, to enhance a deeper understanding of current social, political and economic relations.

In this concluding section, our purpose is to present a brief overview of what the selected influential thinkers add to our understanding about the changing institutions, dynamics and outcomes of capitalism. The following brief overview points out to the reader the main tenets of the selected authors' ideas in order to enhance the enlargement of current debates on proposals that aim to transform contemporary economic and social life in more sustainable and more just.

Karl Polanyi (1886-1964)

Throughout the First Industrial Revolution, economic, social and cultural transformations turned out to subordinate social relations to the market economy. The economic changes that resulted from the Industrial Revolution cannot be apprehended if ignoring the political, social and ethical issues. In this setting, the commodity fiction is the vital organizing process in the market economy. Labour, land and money are commodities in a context where social life is embedded in the economy rather than the economy embedded in social life. In other words, the economic motive overwhelms social life. Although the double movement refers to the institutionalization of the market economy, Polanyi highlights the historical emergence of mechanisms of social protection to face the harmful social effects of the institutional set-up of the free-markets that, in his own words, seems to be is a "satanic mill".

Rudolf Hilferding (1877-1944)

Britain's international role in the world began to erode, even though it still remained important as an international trade and banker, after the Second Industrial Revolution. This new historical phase is called as Monopolist Capitalism since the real-world economy is characterized by the capital concentration and centralization in industrial markets that is leveraged by financial institutions. Financial capital reveals the inherent tendency of capital accumulation towards the predominance of interest-bearing capital. The new business trends expresses the expansion of financial capital with the growth of joint-stock corporations that fosters industrial monopolization. In this context of monopolization, as Hilferding highlights, financial capital increasingly expands its power over business and has deep influence on market structures and the evolution of demand and national income.

Eric Hobsbawm (1917-2012)

In the nineteenth century, the Pax Britannica was a period associated with the hegemony of the British Empire. During this period, there was a classic division between an industrialized centre and a producing periphery of raw materials. The British economy was a central element in the development of the nineteenth-century world economy. In the 1880s, Britain consumed almost half of the world-wide traded wheat and meat and bought most of the tea and raw cotton, besides 35% of the wood. In the context of the Second Industrial Revolution, the control over the international markets was redefined. This period of national rivalries and neocolonialism expressed the conflicts that arose from the reorganization of manufacturing and trade flows at the system level. In the mid 1950s, the American hegemony changed the world order. After World War II, a redefinition of international trade agreements favoured a gradual liberalization of international trade flows. Throughout this period, American corporations enhanced inter and intra-firm international trade flows. There was a generalization of the American growth model's main features: industrialization, urbanization, mass consumption, cheap energy (oil). Within this setting, development strategies were linked to the coordination of economic policies to foster growth by nation–states. After the 1970s, the influence of globalization over the economic, social, cultural and political life has spread, as Hobswam shows, huge challenges, including weak economic growth, higher income inequality, violence, civil conflicts and wars in a context where nation-states seem to be unable to face social needs and the maintenance of public order.

Karl Marx (1818-1883)

The capitalist economic system is based on a mode of production for trade in the markets where workers are formally free persons. However, the subordination of labour to capital is at the centre of the capitalist mode of production. Workers produce a surplus as they work more than the socially necessary labour time and capitalists exploit the working class by extracting surplus value from its labour. As a result, the progressive movement of capital can be referred as "money generating money". The real subsumption of labour under capital means the subordination of human beings, on a large scale, to machinery, that is to say, to capitalist production. In this setting, Marx highlights the alienating effects of the real subsumption of labour that turn out to overwhelm all social dynamics.

Michal Kalecki (1899-1970)

The Kaleckian theory of effective demand refers to the relationship between spending, production, prices and income distribution. In this approach, the variables of spending (capitalist consumption, investment and consumption of workers) are related to economic sectors of integrated production. There are three economic sectors of vertically integrated production, which produce respectively: capital goods (D1); consumer goods for capitalists (D2) and consumer goods for workers (D3). At the same time, in each economic sector, income is distributed in the form of profits (P1, P2 and P3) and wages (W1, W2, W3). The factors affecting income distribution include: the degree of monopoly; the ratio of the costs of raw materials and labour costs, and the composition of the industrial structure. As Kalecki emphasizes, the evolution of priced depends on firms' market power, which in turn is affected by industrial concentration. The price formation in market structures where firms hold market power to fix their prices above direct costs (wages and raw materials) reveals the power of concentrated capital over labour and society.

John Kenneth Galbraith (1908-2006)

After the middle 1950s, the modern industrial system refers to the group of corporations that has control of a large part of the output produced in key sectors of the economy. Within these corporations, the technostructure controls the industrial shareholders and plan the long-term growth of the corporation. This technostructure does not act to maximize profits, but principally to maintain the organization in the market and to ensure its further expansion by using retained profits. He shows how these organizations develop informal practices of pricing, in conjunction with strategies of marketing, advertisement, research & development to favour the feasibility of long-term planning. Considering the market power of large corporations in the modern industrial system, Galbraith's highlights the set of deep interconnections between large corporations and governments.

Eugene von Böhm-Bawerk (1851-1914)

The concept of utility is at the centre of the theory of value since the marginal utility of any good determines its value. According to this subjective theory of value, the marginal utility refers to the amount of utility that an individual gets with the consumption of additional units of a good. However, the value of a good is dependant on the interaction between *want* and *provision*. In other words, the price or exchange value of a good is the result of the competitive forces of supply and demand. He shows the role of inter-temporal allocation and of the degree of roundaboutness of production in the analysis of the rate of interest. Böhm-Bawerk highlights the valuation of present and future goods and concludes that the rate of interest is determined, on the supply side, by time preference and, on the demand side, on the productiveness. In his view, the level of interest rate of equilibrium is determined by real factors.

John Maynard Keynes (1883-1914)

In a monetary economy of production, money links the present and the future. Money is the asset has the highest degree of liquidity. The higher degree of liquidity of a non-monetary asset depends on the possibility of converting this asset into cash at lower transaction costs in a particular period of time. Among non-monetary asset, investment refers to: i) spending on capital goods, also called fixed capital, such as the purchase of plant and equipment either to replace existing capacity that is depreciating or to increase capacity; ii) inventories that firms hold to satisfy miscalculated demand on the final goods they produce. Aggregate investment is an autonomous form of spending and its level is mainly conditioned by expected profits, the level of interest rates and business conventions. In a dynamic perspective, consumption and investment are linked through flows of income: changes in the level of investment spending provoke changes in the level of income and consumption. On behalf of the uncertain future and the alternatives of wealth accumulation, investment is the most volatile component of gross domestic output. Considering the instability of income in the capitalist system and the structural presence of involuntary unemployment, Keynes highlights the role of anti-cyclical government interventions to manage aggregate demand by monetary and fiscal policies.

James Tobin (1918-2002)

In the process of money creation, bank strategies and central banks' instruments and policies are intertwined. Also known as the monetary base, the high powered money corresponds to notes and coins that perform the payment functions by virtue of legal tender status. Under the central bank monopoly of issuance, the monetary base is a claim that general public, government and banks have on the central bank. The monetary base is considered to be part of the liabilities at the central bank balance sheet in the form of currency in circulation, cash hold by public outside the banking system, and bank reserves, either vault cash at commercial banks or commercial banks' deposits at the central bank (required and voluntary reserves). In the process of money creation, the monetary base is also called high-powered money because of the magnifying effects of its changes on the quantity of money supply through the money multiplier. Considering this setting, Tobin highlights that money bank creation is a driver of economic growth and speculation in the contemporary capitalist system where banks are profit-seeking agents tat manage complex portfolios of assets and liabilities.

Alfred Marshall (1842-1924)

In a perfect market, the price (value) of any good is determined at the equilibrium point of its demand and supply. In other words, the price (value) of any good is determined by the economic forces that condition the behaviour of supply and demand at the margin. Indeed, the marginal utility of a good and the marginal cost of production govern the value of a good in a perfect market. Time and space are relevant in the analysis of prices. For instance, the market price of a good may be defined as the price ruling at a particular period if time where the supply is fixed and the price depends mainly on demand. Besides, in the short-run, the amount of variable inputs can change and the fixed plants remain constant and in the case of long-run periods, not only the amount of variable inputs can change, but also the size and features of the plants. Marshall's analysis of markets and prices shows that Economics is the study of human beings that aims to explain the ordinary business of life oriented to the satisfaction of their needs.

Joan Robinson (1903-1983)

A market is considered imperfect when consumers have different scales of preferences between firms that produce the same good. Under imperfect competition, the demand curve for a good of an individual firm slopes downward and the price of the good is greater than marginal revenue since the price elasticity of demand is less than infinite. Besides, imperfect market competition will also arise when the participation of the output of one firm in the total output of the industry is high. In this setting, normal profits refer to the level of profits that occur when there is no trend for changes in the number of firms in an industry. In the real-world, as the level of normal profits depends on the conditions of the firms' supply, normal profits could differ according to the scales of production of the firms in the same industry and across industries. Robinson shows how, in imperfect markets, managerial decisions, that include price discrimination and market segmentation, are practices aimed to increase market share and profits. Consequently, the market power of these firms tuns out to reinforce unfair competition.

Milton Friedman (1912-2006)

In the late 1960, monetarism restates the quantity theory of money as a theory of money demand and price stability as the main target of economic policy. Central Banks should follow monetary rules to control the quantity of money supply and, therefore, to avoid the emergence of inflationary pressures. Considering the Phillips curve – that shows an inverse relation between unemployment and the rate of change of nominal wages (or prices) – Friedman proposes a short-term and long –term theoretical approach about the relation between inflation and unemployment. Until today, the non-accelerating inflation rate of unemployment (NAIRU) is considered in policy issues: it is the level of unemployment level determined by real factors that does not put upward pressures on inflation.

Adam Smith (1723-1780)

At the time of Smith, the English government extensively controlled foreign trade, prices and wages. Smith rejected the Mercantilist agenda that proposed the accumulation of gold and silver, a favourable balance of trade through increasing exports, expansion of foreign markets for English manufactured goods, high tariffs to protect the domestic industry, expansion of foreign trade to provide raw materials and a strong merchant marine. Smith was influenced by the age of Enlightenment –historical period overwhelmed by the faith in human reason. The doctrine of the laissez-faire, a product of the Enlightenment, proposed the expansion of free markets and the end of the control of the government on foreign trade. In this setting, Smith proposes that the wealth of a nation should be measured by the total of its production and commerce. In his analysis of the roots of the expansion of the manufacturing system, he highlights the role of the division and specialization of labour on productivity and the growth of free markets.

Joseph Schumpeter (1883-1950)

The Schumpeterian entrepreneur is the one who introduces new products or processes in the markets by new combinations of ideas, factors of production, inputs and technological resources, for instance. The outcomes and linkages of the cyclical clusters of innovations are qualitative and structural changes in markets and industries. In this setting, the emergence of the innovative entrepreneur is associated with new social and economic facts associated with the process of capitalist creative destruction understood as a discontinuous process of development. Schumpeter's ideas on the role of innovative entrepreneurs in the development of the capitalist system have influenced the policy agenda of many developed and developing countries in order to enhance technological innovation in small business, mainly startups.

Hyman Minsky (1919-1996)

The Wall Street paradigm is based on the existence of a monetary economy based on credit relations, organized markets of financial assets, speculation and uncertainty. In this monetary economy, there is a set of interrelated balance sheets and cash flows between income-producing firms, financial institutions and central banks. These relations influence the valuation of the stock of capital assets, the evolution of credit and the pace of investment. Throughout the business cycles, the portfolio structure of firms can be *hedge* (firms can payback debts and cover the interest and principal of the debt from current cash flows); *speculative* (the current cash flow of firms can cover the interest due, but the firm must regularly re-borrow the amount of the principal) or *Ponzi* (the current cash flow of firms is not sufficient to cover the interest or principal due). According to Minsky, the financial fragility hypothesis emphasizes the active role of central banks and financial institutions in shaping the cyclical path of growth in contemporary economies.

David Ricardo (1772-1823)

Free trade, as a normative aspect of the theory, is a principle that allows the market exchanges of goods between countries to be guided by the specialization in production. Ricardo believes that, in the context of free trade, the exchange of goods between countries results from the differences in the costs of production. In his classical example, he shows that being the labour costs associated with the production of wine lower in Portugal than the labour costs in England for the same end, Portugal presents a comparative advantage for the production of wine and England for the production of cloth. In Ricardos' view, free trade is mutually beneficial for all countries engaged in foreign trade and capital mobility equalizes the rate of profits between countries.

Friedreich von Hayek (1899-1992)

According to Hayek, the coordination of multiple and independent individual plans and decisions is the fundamental problem in Economics. Only the competitive price market system can achieve such coordination since rational economic agents consider that market prices are signals that reveal relevant market information to make economic calculations. To preserve the competitive order, Hayek rejected the Keynesian agenda of government interventions and he even proposed the denationalization of money in the 1970s. In his view, no government can gather sufficient information in order to elaborate future plans for the economy and society. Besides, political pressures usually misguide policy interventions' targets. Under the neo-liberal agenda, his recommendation for emphasizing price stability in policy making has been globally adopted.

Robert Mundell (1932-)

The evolution of the international monetary system has been characterized by the adoption of different exchange rate regimes and by different degrees of international capital mobility across countries. Considering the changing international institutional set-up, Mundell highlights the influence of the type of exchange rate regime and the degree of international capital mobility on the efficiency of monetary and fiscal policies to accomplish increases in aggregate income in open economies. Among the conclusions of his model: i) in the context of a fixed exchange rate regime and high international capital mobility, the management of fiscal policy can increase the levels of aggregate income; and ii) under floating exchange rates and high capital mobility, the management of monetary policy is efficient to increase the levels of aggregate demand. After the crisis of the Bretton Woods system in the early 1970s, Mundell`s analysis on the macroeconomic challenges in open economies and currency areas proved to be increasingly relevant to policy makers.

Arthur Pigou (1877-959)

According to Pigou's analysis on welfare, each individual in society attempts to maximize the satisfaction or utility from his expenditure on different goods and services. Different people derive the same satisfaction or utility out of the same real income. Satisfactions or utilities can be compared across people considering that the gain in utility of an additional amount of income to a poor man is greater than the loss of utility to a rich man from the same amount of income. In this setting, social welfare is regarded as the aggregation of individual welfares. In Pigou's view, national income growth generally results social welfare improvement if it does not reduce the share of income of the poor people. Any income redistribution that favours poor people without reduction in national income improves social welfare. His mainly contribution to welfare shows that the existence of negative or positive externalities in production is a sufficient justification for government intervention by means of taxes or subsidies. Until today, the Pigouvian tax is considered to be an efficient policy instrument to face negative externalities.

Amartya Sen (1933-)

According to Sen, income inequality, health, education, unemployment and social exclusion should be integrated into a multifaceted analysis of well-being. Departing from this idea, the capability approach focuses on the actual ability to do different things that a person values doing. In other words, capability is the aspect of freedom related to individual substantive opportunities in society. Mainly concerned about the deep connection between Economics and Justice, Sen's contribution to the theory of social choice opened space towards the study of rules for collective decisions to shape policy interventions oriented not only to expand human capabilities of all members of society but also to face the demand for justice, such as the demand for sustainable development. In the attempt to formulate a theory of justice that aims at the formulation of new policy strategies and interventions, Sen argues for a renewal of the bond between the two disciplines: philosophy and economics.

Elinor Ostrom (1933-2012)

According to Ostrom, social-ecological systems are complex systems that couple natural and human systems. Departing from this idea, she builds a theoretical approach to the management of common-pool resources at local and global levels. Common or common-pool resources as public goods with finite benefits. Therefore, common-pool resources can be potentially used beyond the limits of sustainability because of the lack of exclusion of users. This creates an incentive for increasing the rate of use of this resource above its physical or biological renewal. Besides, common property is a kind of institutional arrangement about ownership and responsibility. Considering this framework, polycentric systems of governance are required to build collective-actions. Indeed, Ostrom highlights that there is one ideal governance regime, but a variety of regimes of governance.

MAPPING PATHS FOR FUTURE DIALOGUES

After the brief overview of the main contributions of selected influential thinkers, we can conclude that the findings depend not only on the questions asked, but also on the facts in dispute and the interests confronted. Besides, the ongoing dialogue in Economics fosters current generations of students and economists to spread the renewal of the bond between philosophy and economics to re-think and expand future dialogues about the following issues:

- Ontological indeterminism that overwhelms market dynamics;
- Epistemological fallibilism in economic knowledge;
- Role of mathematics in realist economic theories;
- Role of induction, deduction and abduction in economic inquiry;
- Realism of economic theories.

Schools of economic thought coexist with ontological, epistemological and methodological differences- such as Neoclassical, Monetarist, Marxist, Iinstitucionalist, Neoricardian, Austrian, Post-Keynesian, Evolutionist, Sraffian, to mention some of the most relevant. Despite such diversification of assumptions and proposals, the Neoclassical has been the dominant theory since the 19th century - both at the academy and in the formulation of policies – and adopts the regularity of the rational behaviour of agents in decision-making as the ontological presupposition about the social reality. From the methodological point of view, this theoretical approach emphasizes the importance of mathematical models as analytical resources. As a result and, mainstream (neoclassical) theoretical models reinforce the logical and deductive mathematical method and turn out to reject the complexity and evolutionary dynamism of the real world.

The global financial crisis of 2007-2008 put in question the assumptions of neoclassical theory and revived the debate over the credentials of this economic theory as a science with predictive power. However, even after the crisis have denounced the gap between reality and the framework of neoclassical economic models, economists of this theoretical dominant school of thought have insisted on the validity of the ergodic axioms for the development of new deterministic models. Indeed, such economists insist on the use of general equilibrium theories that seek to explain the behaviour of economic relations using deterministic models.

We can identify a relevant feature of the crisis in current economic knowledge by reference to the insistence on the determination of the object of investigation of Economics - matter that became known as the Ricardian Vice. This term, which refers to the English Economist David Ricardo, was coined by Joseph A.

Schumpeter in his book *History of Economic Analysis* when he criticized the "habit" assigned to Ricardo to present simplified assumptions to represent the economy as a whole and as the basis of practical economic solutions in tautologies.

Indeed, Schumpeter rejected, in the process of formulation of economic theories, the use of simplifying assumptions as the basis for the construction of reasoning that favour causality relations because this "habit" - the Ricardian Vice- generates analytical results of tautological nature that lack of practical importance to solve economic problems. By rejecting the Ricardian Vice, Schumpeter emphasizes the complexity and indeterminacy of the object of investigation of economic sciences.

The changing environment of economic activities and behaviour of agents throughout cronological time -that is irreversible- refers to a certain degree of indeterminacy associated with the specificities and the evolution of the economic system where the standards of behaviour are complex and interrelated variables influence the economic, social and political context. Such lack of precision makes innocuous the procedures often used by economists who have built and used economic models in which both the ontological uncertainty about epistemological uncertainty are not considered.

In this regard, Schumpeter criticizes the behaviour of economists who use a hypothetical-deductive logic in the construction of knowledge in Economics. In other words, his criticism is addressed to those who believe to understand the essential aspects of economic reality from a strictly logical method- which ultimately privilege mathematical modelling and hypothetical-deductive approaches.

However, economists that privilege deductive methods of inquiry in Economics, have caused, by omission and, as a result, the risk of adopting a proper nominalist bias in the formulation of economic concepts. Today, the intense concern about problems of method in Economics strengthens that mentioned nominalism. As a result, the dialogue with the reality ends up being rejected in a context where mathematical models based on the "ideology" of the individual rational or with limited rationality have been spread.

Such bias would not reveal a realism that would address the general nature of the possibilities of the object of investigation in Economics, which would shape the nature of economic theories to be adopted. Given the nature of the object of investigation in Economics, that displays a multitude of variables, and is subject to a high degree of indeterminacy, casualties cannot be taken as causalities. In this sense, a deterministic ontology does not seem to cope with the complexity of the economic phenomena.

As John Maynard Keynes warned, uncertainty and randomness are inherent to economic phenomena. As a result, the interpretation of the economic phenomena demands not only purely deductive logic, but also other forms of inquiry. To reject the axiom of ergodicity of neoclassical theories, Keynes criticizes the predetermination of the future and, consequently, the power of prediction of probability distribution analysis when applied to the decision making process in an uncertain world.

Therefore, a certain degree of indeterminacy of the economic phenomena should be considered in the formulation of economic theories. The acceptance of a certain degree of indeterminacy in economic phenomena reinforces the importance of formulating realistic economic theories that consider the economic system as a dynamic and evolving process where chance and economic laws are intertwined. Indeed, these realist theories are required to propose new solutions to face the current deep social and economic challenges in the context of globalization.

FURTHER READING

Blancas A. The Ricardian Vice: A Schumpeter's observation 2012. European Association for Evolutionary Political economy. Papers in Evolutionary Political Economy, 8. http://eaepe.econ.tuwien.ac.at/pepe/papers/Blancas_2012.pdf

Bronx R. Epistemological difficulties with neo-classical economics 2011. Conference Paper. London School of Economics and Political Science. http://eprints.lse.ac.uk/39423/1/Epistemological_difficulties_with_neoclassical_economies_(LSERO).pdf

Davidson Paul. 2012. Is economics a science? Should economics be rigorous?. *Real-world economics review*, 59, pp. 58-66.

Davis J. Davidson, Non-Ergodicity and Individuals. In: Davidson P, Arestis P, Eds. Methodology, Theory and Policy in Keynes: Essays in Honour of Paul Davidson. Cheltenham, UK: Edward Elgar Publishing 1998; Vol. 3: pp. 1-16.

Gambina J. La crisis de la economía mundial y los desafíos para el pensamiento crítico. In: Gambina J, Ed. La crisis capitalista y sus alternativas. Buenos Aires: CLACSO 2010; pp. 77-92.

Garnett R. Pluralism, Academic Freedom, and Heterodox Economics. Rev Radic Polit Econ 2011; 43(4): 562-7.
[http://dx.doi.org/10.1177/0486613411402647]

Gillies D. Economics and Research Assessment Systems. Economic Thought 2012; 1(1): 23-47.

Fullbrook E, Ed. Ontology and Economics: Tony Lawson and His Critics. UK: Routledge 2009.

Hausman D. Ontology and Methodology in Economics. Econ Philos 1999; 15(2)
[http://dx.doi.org/10.1017/S0266267100004028]

Hodgson G M. Generalized Darwinism and Evolutionary Economics: From Ontology to Theory. Biol Theory 2011; 6(4): 326-37.
[http://dx.doi.org/10.1007/s13752-012-0043-5]

Kurt D, Potts J. Evolutionary Realism: A New Ontology for Economics. J Econ Methodol 2004; 11(2)

Mäki U, Ed. The Economic World View: Studies in the Ontology of Economics. UK: Cambridge University Press 2001.

[http://dx.doi.org/10.1017/CBO9780511752049]

Morgan J. Seeing the Potential of Realism in Economics. Philos Soc Sci 2015; 45(2): 176-201. [http://dx.doi.org/10.1177/0048393114530785]

Hands DW. Reflection without Rules: Economic Methodology and Contemporary Science Theory. Cambridge: Cambridge University Press 2001. [http://dx.doi.org/10.1017/CBO9780511612602]

Lawson T. Mathematical Modelling and Ideology in the Economics Academy: competing explanations of the failings of the modern discipline? Economic Thought 2012; 1(1): 3-22.

Madi MA, Reardon J. The economics curriculum: towards a radical reformulation. UK: World Economics Associaton and College Publications 2014.

McCloskey D. The Rhetoric of Economics. J Econ Lit 1983; 21(2): 481-517.

Dolphin T, Nash D, Eds. Complex New World Translating new economic thinking into public policy. Londres: IPPR 2012.

Wible JR. The Economics of Science: Methodology and Epistemology as if Economics Really Mattered. New York: Routledge 1998. [http://dx.doi.org/10.4324/9780203176979]

ABBREVIATIONS

BIS = Bank of International Settlements

CEO = Chief Executive Officer

CSR = Corporate Social Responsibility

ECB = European Central Bank

FED = Federal Reserve System

ILO = International Labor Organization

IMF = International Monetary Fund

IUF = International Union of Food, Agricultural, Hotel, Restaurant, Catering, Tobacco and Allied Workers' Associations

LSE = Londos School of Economics and Political Science

M&A = Mergers and acquisitions

NAIRU = Non-accelerating rate of unemployment

OECD = Organization for Economic Cooperation and Development

PK = Post Keynesian

R&D = Research and Development

SEEA = System of Environmental and Economic Accounts

SEEAF = Sytem of Environmental and Economic Accounting for Fisheries

SEEA-MFA = System of Environmental-Economic Accounting for Material Flow Accounts

SEEAW = System of Environmental-Economic Accounting for Water

TPP = Trans-Pacific Partnership

UN = United Nations

UN COP = United Nations Conference of Parties

UNCEEA = United Nations Committee of Experts on Environmental-Economic Accounting

UNSD = United Nations Statistics Division

UK = United Kingdom

U.S. = United States

Worl War I = First World War

Wold War II = Second World War

BIBLIOGRAPHY

Böhm-Bawerk, E. (1884). *Capital and Interest.* Retrieved from: https://mises.org/system/tdf/Capital%20and%20Interest.pdf?file=1&type=document

Böhm-Bawerk, E. (1889). *The Positive Theory of Capital.* Retrieved from: https://mises.org/library/positive-theory-capital

Böhm-Bawerk, E. (1896). *Karl Marx and the Close of his System.* London: Fisher Unwin, 1898. https://mises.org/library/karl-marx-and-close-his-system

Friedman, M. (1948). A Monetary and Fiscal Framework for Economic Stability. *Am. Econ. Rev, 38*(3), 245-264.

Friedman, M. (1951). Some Comments on the Significance of Labour Unions for Economic Policy. In: Wright, D., (Ed.), *The Impact of the Union.* New York: Harcourt Brace.

Friedman, M. (1952). Price, Income, and Monetary Changes in Three Wartime Periods. *Am. Econ. Rev, 42*(2), 612-625.

Friedman, M. (1953). *Essays in Positive Economics.* Chicago, London: Chicago University Press. a

Friedman, M. (1953). Economic Advice and Political Limitations: Rejoinder. *Rev. Econ. Stat, 35*(3), 252. b [http://dx.doi.org/10.2307/1925925]

Friedman, M. (1956). The Quantity Theory of Money –A Restatement. *M. Friedman, Studies in the Quantity Theory of Money.* Chicago: University of Chicago Press.

Friedman, M. (1957). *A theory of the consumption function. NBER General Series 63.* Princeton: Princeton University Press.

Friedman, M. (1959). The Demand for Money: Some Theoretical and Empirical Results. *J. Polit. Econ, 67*(4), 327-351.
[http://dx.doi.org/10.1086/258194]

Friedman, M. (1961). The Lag in Effect of Monetary Policy. *J. Polit. Econ, 69*(5), 447-466.
[http://dx.doi.org/10.1086/258537]

Friedman, M. (1962). *Price Theory, a Provisional Text.* Chicago: Aldine Pub. Co..

Friedman, M. (1962). *Capitalism and Freedom.* Chicago: University of Chicago Press.

Friedman, M., Schwartz, A.J. (1963). *A Monetary History of the United States, 1867-1960. NBER Studies in business cycles no. 12.* Princeton: Princeton University Press.

Friedman, M., Friedman, R. (1981). *Free to Choose: A Personal Statement.* Ringwood, Vic.: Penguin Australia.

Friedman, M., Friedman, R.D. (1998). *Two Lucky People.* Chicago: Chicago University Press.

Galbraith, J.K. (1938). *Modern Competition and Business Policy.* Oxford: Oxford University Press.

Galbraith, J.K. (1980). *A Theory of Price Control.* Cambridge, MA: Harvard University Press. (Original work published 1952)
[http://dx.doi.org/10.4159/harvard.9780674333048]

Galbraith, J.K. (1993). *American Capitalism: The Concept of Countervailing Power.* London: Transaction Publishers. (Original work published 1952)

Galbraith, J.K. (1958). *The Affluent Society.* London: Penguin Books.

Galbraith, J.K. (2007). *The New Industrial State.* Princeton, NJ: Princeton University Press. (Original work published 1967)

Galbraith, J.K. (1973). *Economics and the Public Purpose.* Boston, MA: Houghton Mifflin.

Galbraith, J.K. (1979). *The Age of Uncertainty.* Boston, MA: Houghton Mifflin. (Original work published 1977)

Galbraith, J.K. (2001). *The Nature of Mass Poverty.* Bridgewater, NJ: Replica Books. (Original work published 1979)

Galbraith, J.K. (1983). *The Anatomy of Power.* Boston, MA: Houghton Mifflin & Co..

Galbraith, J.K. (1997). *The Good Society: The Humane Agenda.* NY: Mariner Books.

Galbraith, J.K. (2004). *The Economics of Innocent Fraud: Truth for our time.* London: Allen Lane.

Hayek, F. (1937). *Individualism and Economic Order.* Chicago: University of Chicago Press.

Hayek, F. (1937). Economics and Knowledge. *Economica, 4*, 33-54.
[http://dx.doi.org/10.2307/2548786]

Hayek, F. (1944). *The Road to Serfdom.* Chicago: University of Chicago Press.

Hayek, F. (1945). The Use of Knowledge in Society. *Am. Econ. Rev, 4*, 519-530.

Hayek, F. (1960). *The Constitution of Liberty.* Chicago: University of Chicago Press.

Hayek, F. (1976). *Denationalisation of Money: The Argument Refined.* London: Institute of Economic Affairs.

Hayek, F. (1974). *The Pretense of Knowledge*. Retrieved from: http://www.nobelprize.org/nobel_prizes/economic-sciences/laureates/1974/hayek-lecture.html

Hayek, F. 1991- 2015 In: Caldwell, B., (Ed.), *The Collected Works of F.A. Hayek.* Chicago: University of Chicago Press.

Hilferding, R. (1920). Retrieved from: https://www.marxists.org/archive/hilferding/1904/criticism/

Hilferding, R. (1905). *Parliamentarianism and the General Strike*. Retrieved from: https://www.marxists.org/archive/hilferding/1905/11/parliamentarianism-strike.htm

Hilferding, R. (1910). *Finance Capital: A Study of the Latest Phase of Capitalist Development*. Retrieved from: https://www.marxists.org/archive/hilferding/1910/finkap/

Hilferding, R. (1933). *Between Decisions.* Retrieved from: https://www.marxists.org/archive/hilferding/1933/decisions.htm

Hilferding, R. (1940). *State Capitalism or Totalitarian State Economy.* Retrieved from: https://www.marxists.org/archive/hilferding/1940/statecapitalism.htm

Hobsbwam, E. (1959). *Primitive Rebels. Studies in Archaic Forms of Social Movement in the 19th and 20th centuries.* New York: Norton Library.

Hobsbwam, E. (1962). The Age of Revolution. *Europe,* 1789-1848. London, UK: Weidenfeld and Nicolson.

Hobsbwam, E. (1976). *The Age of Capital: 1848-1875, 1975. London: Weidenfeld and Nicolson.* New. York: Charles Scribner's Sons.

Hobsbwam, E. (1989). *The Age of Empire: 1875-1914. London: George. Weidenfeld and Nicolson.* New York: Pantheon Books.

Hobsbwam, E. (1990). *Nations and Nationalism since 1780, Programme, Myth, Reality.* Cambridge: Cambridge University Press.

Hobsbwam, E. (1994). *The Age of Extremes. The short twentieth century 1914-1991.* London: Penguin.

Hobsbwam, E. (2002). *Interesting Times: A Twentieth-Century life.* London: Allen Lane.

Hobsbwam, E. (2007). *Globalisation, Democracy and Terrorism.* London: Abacus.

Hobsbwam, E. (2011). *How to Change the World: Tales of Marx and Marxism.* Retrieved from: http://ouleft.org/wp-content/uploads/How_to_Change_the_World_Hobsbawm.pdf

Hobsbwam, E. (2013). *Fractured Times: Culture and Society in the 20th Century.* London: Little, Brown.

Kalecki, M. (1939). *Essays in the Theory of Economic Fluctuations.* London: Allen & Unwin.

Kalecki, M. (1943). Political Aspects of Full Employment. *Polit. Q, 4*, 322-331.
[http://dx.doi.org/10.1111/j.1467-923X.1943.tb01016.x]

Kalecki, M. (1943). *Studies in Economic Dynamics.* London: Allen & Unwin.

Kalecki, M. (1954). *Theory of Economic Dynamics: An essay on cyclical and long-run changes in capitalist economy.* London: Allen & Unwin.

Kalecki, M. (1962). Observations on the Theory of Growth. *Econ. J, 47*, 134-153.
[http://dx.doi.org/10.2307/2228620]

Kalecki, M. (1970). Theories of Growth in Different Social Systems. *Scientia,* (May-June), 311-161.

Kalecki, M. (1971). *Selected Essays on the Dynamics of the Capitalist Economy, 1933-1970.* Cambridge: Cambridge University Press.

Kalecki, M. (1990). Capitalism: Business Cycles and Full Employment. In: Osiatynski, J., (Ed.), *Collected Works of Michal Kalecki* (Vol. Vol. 1). Oxford: Oxford University Press.

Kalecki, M. (1991). Capitalism: Economic Dynamics. In: Osiatynski, J., (Ed.), *Collected Works of Michal Kalecki* (Vol. Vol. 2). Oxford: Oxford University Press.

Kalecki, M. (1997). Studies in Applied Economics. In: Osiatynski, J., (Ed.), *Collected Works of Michal Kalecki* (Vol. Vol. 3). Oxford: Oxford University Press.

Keynes, J.M. (1912). *Indian Currency and Finance*. Retrieved from: https://archive.org/details/IndianCurrencyAndFinance

Keynes, J.M. (1921). *A Treatise on Probability*. Retrieved from: ftp://ftp.informatik.rwth-aachen.de/pub/mirror/ibiblio/gutenberg/3/2/6/2/32625/32625-pdf.pdf

Keynes, J.M. (1923). *A Tract on Monetary Reform*. Retrieved from: http://delong. typepad.com/keynes-192--a-tract-on-monetary-reform.pdf

Keynes, J.M. (1930). *A Treatise on Money*. Retrieved from: http://www.gbv.de/dms/zbw/730404803.pdf

Keynes, J.M. (1936). *The General Theory of Employment, Interest and Money*. Retrieved from: http://cas2.umkc.edu/economics/people/facultypages/kregel/courses/econ645/winter2011/generaltheory.pdf

Keynes, J.M. (1937). The General Theory of Unemployment. *Q. J. Econ, 51*(2), 209-223. [http://dx.doi.org/10.2307/1882087]

Keynes, J.M. (1940). How to Pay for the War. In *The Collected Writings of John Maynard Keynes*, Vol. 9: Essays in Persuasion (367-439). London and Basingstoke: Macmillan.

Keynes, J.M. (1973a). The General Theory and After. Part I Preparation. In *The Collected Writings of John Maynard Keynes*. Vol.13. London and Basingtoke: Macmillan.

Keynes, J.M. (1973b). The General Theory and After, Part II Defence and Development. In *The Collected Writings of John Maynard Keynes*. Vol.14. London and Basingtoke: Macmillan.

Marshall, A. (1898). Distribution and exchange. *Econ. J, 8*(29), 37-59. [http://dx.doi.org/10.2307/2956696]

Marshall, A. (1890). *Principles of economics*. Retrieved from: http://www.econlib.org/library/Marshall/marP.html

Marshall, A. (1892). *Elements of industry*. Retrieved from: https://archive.org/details/elementsofeconom00marsuoft

Marshall, A. (1903). *The new Cambridge curriculum in Economics and associated branches of Political Science: its purpose and plan*. Retrieved from: https://archive.org/details/newcambridgecurr00marsuoft

Marshall, A. (1906). *Introduction to the tripos in economics and associated branches of political science*. Retrieved from: https://archive.org/stream/introductiontotr00mars/introductiontotr00mars_djvu.txt

Marshall, A. (1919). *Industry and Trade: A Study of Industrial Technique and Business Organization*. Retrieved from: http://socserv.mcmaster.ca/econ/ugcm/3ll3/marshall/Industry&Trade.pdf

Marshall, A. (1923). *Money, Credit and Commerce*. London: MacMillan.

Marshall, A. (1925). *Memorials of Alfred Marshall*. London: Macmillan.

Marshall, A. (1975). *The Early Economic Writings*. London, Basingstoke: Macmillan.

Marshall, A. (1996). *Official papers of Alfred Marshall: a supplement, 1842-1924*. Cambridge, New York:

Cambridge University Press for the Royal Economic Society.
[http://dx.doi.org/10.1017/CBO9780511559471]

Marx, K. (1844). *Economic and Philosophic Manuscripts of 1844*. Retrieved from: https://www.marxists.org/archive/marx/works/1844/manuscripts/preface.htm

Marx, K. (1845). *The German Ideology*. Retrieved from: https://www.marxists.org/archive/marx/works/1845/german-ideology/index.htm

Marx, K. (1847). *Wage, Labour and Capital*. Retrieved from: https://www.marxists.org/archive/marx/works/1847/wage-labour/index.htm

Marx, K. (1848). *Manifesto of the Communist Party*. Retrieved from: https://www.marxists.org/archive/marx/works/1847/wage-labour/index.htm

Marx, K. (1857). Retrieved from: https://www.marxists.org/archive/marx/works/download/Marx_Grundrisse.pdf

Marx, K. (1859). *A Contribution to the Critique of Political Economy*. Retrieved from: https://www.marxists.org/archive/marx/works/download/Marx_Contribution_to_the_Critique_of_Political_Economy.pdf

Marx, K. (1862). Retrieved from: http://www.bard.edu/library/arendt/pdfs/Marx-Surplus.pdf

Marx, K. (1867). *Capital*, Volume I. Retrieved from: https://www.marxists.org/archive/marx/works/1867-c1/index.htm

Marx, K. (1885). *Capital*, Volume II (posthumously published by F. Engels). Retrieved from: https://www.marxists.org/archive/marx/works/download/Marx_Capital_Vol_2.pdf)

Marx, K. (1894). *Capital*, Volume III (posthumously published by F. Engels). Retrieved from: https://www.marxists.org/archive/marx/works/download/Marx_Capital_Vol_3.pdf

Minsky, H.P. (1975). *John Maynard Keynes*. London: Macmillan.
[http://dx.doi.org/10.1007/978-1-349-02679-1]

Minsky, H.P. (1976). *A Theory of Systemic Fragility*. Retrieved from: http://digitalcommons.bard.edu/cgi/viewcontent.cgi?article=1230&context=hm_archive

Minsky, H.P. (1980). Money, Financial Markets, and the Coherence of a Market Economy. *J. Post Keynes. Econ, 3*(1), 21-31.
[http://dx.doi.org/10.1080/01603477.1980.11489192]

Minsky, H.P. (1982). *Can "It" Happen Again? Essays on Instability and Finance*. Armonk: M.E. Sharpe.

Minsky, H.P. (1986). *Stabilizing an Unstable Economy*. New Haven, Connecticut: Yale University Press.

Minsky, H.P. (1991). *Financial crises: systemic or idiosyncratic*. 51. Retrieved from: http://www.levyinstitute.org/pubs/wp51.pdf

Minsky, H.P. (1996). *Uncertainty and the Institutional Structure of Capitalist Economies*. Retrieved from: http://www.levyinstitute.org/pubs/wp155.pdf
[http://dx.doi.org/10.1080/00213624.1996.11505800]

Minsky, H.P. (1992). *The Financial Instability Hypothesis*. Retrieved from: http://www.levyinstitute.

org/pubs/wp74.pdf

Minsky, H.P. (1993). On the non-neutrality of money. Quarterly Review, Federal Reserve Bank of New York, issue Spr, 77-82.

Mundell, R.A. (1961). A Theory of Optimum Currency Areas. *Am. Econ. Rev, 51*, 657-665.

Mundell, R.A. (1963). Capital Mobility and Stabilization Policy under Fixed and Flexible Exchange Rates. *Can. J. Econ, 29*, 475-485.

Mundell, R.A. (1968). *International Economics.* New York: MacMillan.

Mundell, R.A. (1968). The Collapse of the Gold Exchange Standard. *Am. J. Agric. Econ, 50*(5), 1123-1134. [http://dx.doi.org/10.2307/1237298]

Mundell, R.A. (1968). *Man and Economics.* New York: McGraw-Hill. c

Mundell, R.A. (1985). *Macropolicies in the World Economy and the New Capitalist Revolution.* Taipei: Institute of Economics, Academia Sinica.

Mundell, R.A. (1997). The International Monetary System in the 21st Century: Could Gold Make a Comeback?. Lecture, St. Vincent College (Latrobe, Pa.), March 12.

Mundell, R.A., Polak, J. (1977). *The New International Monetary System.* New York: Columbia University Press.

Ostrom, E. (1987). Institutional Arrangements for Resolving the Commons Dilemma: Some Contending Approaches. In: McCay, B.J., Acheson, J.M., (Eds.), *The Question of the Commons: The Culture and Ecology of Communal Resources* (pp. 250-265). Tucson: University of Arizona Press.

Ostrom, E. (1990). *Governing the Commons: The Evolution of Institutions for Collective Action.* New York: Cambridge University Press.
[http://dx.doi.org/10.1017/CBO9780511807763]

Ostrom, E. (2007). A diagnostic approach for going beyond panaceas. *Proc. Natl. Acad. Sci. USA, 104*(39), 15181-15187.
[http://dx.doi.org/10.1073/pnas.0702288104] [PMID: 17881578]

Ostrom, E. (2009). A general framework for analyzing sustainability of social-ecological systems. *Science, 325*(5939), 419-422.
[http://dx.doi.org/10.1126/science.1172133] [PMID: 19628857]

Ostrom, E. (2012). Polycentric Systems: Multilevel Governance Involving a Diversity of Organizations. In: Brousseau, E., Dedeurwaerdere, T., (Eds.), *P-A Jouvet & M. Willinger, Global Environmental Commons: Analytical and Political Challenges in Building Governance Mechanisms.* Cambridge, MA: Oxford University Press.
[http://dx.doi.org/10.1093/acprof:oso/9780199656202.003.0005]

Poteete, A.R., Janssen, M.A., Ostrom, E. (2010). *Working Together: Collective Action, the Commons, and Multiple Methods in Practice.* Princeton, NJ: Princeton University Press.
[http://dx.doi.org/10.1515/9781400835157]

Pigou, A.C. (1904). Monopoly and Consumers' Surplus. *Econ. J, 14*, 388-394.
[http://dx.doi.org/10.2307/2221361]

Pigou, A.C. (1912). *Wealth and Welfare.* Retrieved from: https://archive.org/details/cu31924032613386

Pigou, A.C. (1920). *The Economics of Welfare.* Retrieved from: http://oll.libertyfund.org/titles/ pigou-th--economics-of-welfare

Pigou, A.C. (1927). *Industrial fluctuations. Lonon.* Macmillan and Co..

Pigou, A.C. (1927). The Law of Diminishing and Increasing Cost. *Econ. J, 37*, 188-197. [http://dx.doi.org/10.2307/2224353]

Pigou, A.C. (1928). *A study in public finance* (2nd ed.). London: Macmillan and Co..

Pigou, A.C. (1928). An Analysis of Supply. *Econ. J, 40*, 79-116.

Pigou, A.C. (1947). Economic Progress in a Stable Environment. *Economica, 14*, 180-188. [http://dx.doi.org/10.2307/2549787]

Pigou, A.C. (1952). *Essays in Economics.* London: Macmillan.

Polanyi, K. (1968). *Primitive, Archaic, and Modern Economies: Essays of Karl Polanyi.* NY: Anchor Books.

Polanyi, K. (1966). *Dahomey and the Slave Trade. An Analysis of an Archaic Economy.* Washington: University of Washington Press.

Polanyi, K. (1977). *The Livelihood of Man.* NY: Academic Press.

Polanyi, K., Lewis, J., Kitchin, D. (1937). *Christianity and the Social Revolution.* London: Victor Gollancz, London.

Polanyi, K., Arensberg, C.M., Pearson, H.W. (1957). *Trade and Markets in the Early Empires. Economies in History and Theory.* Glencoe: The Free Press.

Polanyi, K., Duczynska, I. (1963). *The Plough and the Pen. Writings from Hungary, 1930-1956.* Toronto: McClelland and Stewart.

Ricardo, D. (1951). *The Works and Correspondence of David Ricardo.* Sraffa with the collaboration of M. H. Dobb (Eds.). Retrieved from: http://oll.libertyfund.org/titles/ricardo-the-works-and- correspondence-o--david-ricardo-11-vols-sraffa-ed

Ricardo, D. (1817). *Principles of Political Economy and Taxation.* Retrieved from: http://oll. libertyfund.org/titles/ricardo-the-works-and-correspondence-of-david-ricardo-vol-1-pr-nciples-of-political-economy-and-taxation

Ricardo, D. (1809). Retrieved from: http://oll.libertyfund.org/titles/ricardo-the-works-and- correspondence-of-david-ricardo-vol-3-pamphlets-and-papers-1809-1811.

Ricardo, D. (1815). Retrieved from: http://oll.libertyfund.org/titles/ricardo-the-works-and- correspondence-of-david-ricardo-vol-4-pamphlets-and-papers-1815-1823

Ricardo, D. (1819). *Speeches and Evidence.* Retrieved from: http://oll.libertyfund.org/ titles/ricardo-th--works-and-correspondence-of-david-ricardo-vol-5-speeches-and-evidence

Ricardo, D. (1815). Retrieved from: http://oll.libertyfund.org/titles/ricardo-the-works-and- correspondence-of-david-ricardo-vol-6-letters-1810-1815

Ricardo, D. (1816). Retrieved from: http://oll.libertyfund.org/titles/ricardo-the-works-and- correspondence-of-david-ricardo-vol-7-letters-1816-1818

Ricardo, D. (1819). Retrieved from: http://oll.libertyfund.org/titles/ricardo-the-works-and- correspondence-of-david-ricardo-vol-8-letters-1819-june-1821

Ricardo, D. (1821). Retrieved from: http://oll.libertyfund.org/titles/ricardo-the-works-and- correspondence-of-david-ricardo-vol-9-letters-1821-1823

Robinson, J. (1932). *Economics as a Serious Subject. The Apologia of an Economist to the Mathematician, the Scientists and the Plain Man.* Cambridge: Heffer.

Robinson, J. (1969). *The Economics of Imperfect Competition* (2nd ed.). London: Macmillan. (Original work published 1933)
[http://dx.doi.org/10.1007/978-1-349-15320-6]

Robinson, J. (1969). *Introduction to the Theory of Employment* (2nd ed.). London: Macmillan. (Original work published 1937)
[http://dx.doi.org/10.1007/978-1-349-00289-4]

Robinson, J. (1947). *Essays in the Theory of Employment* (2nd ed.). Oxford: Basil Blackwell. (Original work published 1937)

Robinson, J. (1851-80). *Collected Economic Papers.* Oxford: Basil Blackwell.

Robinson, J. (1965). *The Accumulation of Capital* (2nd ed.). London: Macmillan. (Original work published 1956)

Robinson, J. (1960). *Exercises in Economic Analysis.* London: Macmillan.

Robinson, J. (1962). *Essays in the Theory of Economic Growth.* London: Macmillan. a
[http://dx.doi.org/10.1007/978-1-349-00626-7]

Robinson, J. (1962). *Economic Philosophy.* Middlesex, England: Penguin.

Robinson, J. (1966). *Economics: An Awkward Corner.* London: George Allen and Unwin.

Robinson, J. (1971). *Economic Heresies.* London, Basingstoke: Macmillan.

Robinson, J. (1978). *Contributions to Modern Economics.* Oxford: Blackwell.

Robinson, J. (1981). *Aspects of Development and Underdevelopment* (2nd ed.). Cambridge: Cambridge University Press. (Original work published 1979)

Robinson, J. (1980). *What Are the Questions? And Other Essays.* Armonk, NY: Sharpe.

Schumpeter, J.A. (1928). The Instability of Capitalism. *Econ. J, 38*, 361-368.
[http://dx.doi.org/10.2307/2224315]

Schumpeter, J. A. (1934). *The Theory Of Economic Development: An Inquiry Into Profits.*

Capital And The Business Cycle. Boston: MA.: Harvard University Press.

Schumpeter, J.A. (1939). *Business Cycles: A Theoretical, Historical and Statistical Analysis of the Capitalist*

Process (Vol. Vol. I and II). New York: MacGraw Hill.

Schumpeter, J.A. (1935). The Analysis of Economic Change. *Rev. Econ. Stat, 17*, 2-10. [http://dx.doi.org/10.2307/1927845]

Schumpeter, J.A. (1942). *Capitalism, Socialism, and Democracy.* NY: Harper & Row.

Schumpeter, J.A. (1951). *Imperialism and Social Classes.* New York: Augustus M. Kelley.

Schumpeter, J.A. (1954). *History of Economic Analysis.* Oxford: Oxford University Press.

Sen, A. (1982). *Choice, Welfare and Measurement.* Oxford: Basil Blackwell. a

Sen, A. (1982). *Poverty and Famines: An Essay on Entitlement and Deprivation.* Oxford: Oxford University Press. b

Sen, A. (1984). Well-Being, Agency and Freedom: The Dewey Lectures. *J. Philos, 82*(4), 169-221.

Sen, A. (1985). *Commodities and Capabilities.* Amsterdam: Elsevier.

Sen, A. (1987). *The Standard of Living.* Cambridge: Cambridge University Press. [http://dx.doi.org/10.1017/CBO9780511570742]

Sen, A. (1988). *On Ethics and Economics.* Oxford: Blackwell Publishing.

Sen, A. (1992). *Inequality Reexamined.* Cambridge, Mass.: Harvard University Press.

Sen, A. (1993). Capability and Well-being. In: Nussbaum, M., Sen, A., (Eds.), *The Quality of Life.* Oxford: Clarendon Press.
[http://dx.doi.org/10.1093/0198287976.003.0003]

Sen, A. (1995). Gender Inequality and Theories of Justice. In: Nussbaum, M., Glover, J., (Eds.), *Women, Culture and Development: A Study of Human Capabilities.* Oxford: Clarendon Press.
[http://dx.doi.org/10.1093/0198289642.003.0011]

Sen, A. (1997). *Resources, Values, and Development.* Massachusetts: Harvard University Press.

Sen, A. (1999). *Development as Freedom.* New York: Knopf Press.

Sen, A. (2002). *Rationality and Freedom.* Cambridge, Massachusetts: Harvard University Press.

Sen, A. (2007). *Identity and Violence: The Illusion of Destiny.* London: Penguin Books Ltd..

Sen, A. (2009). *The Idea of Justice.* London: Penguin Books Ltd..

Sen, A. (2010). The Place of Capability in a Theory of Justice. In: Brighouse, H., Robeyns, I., (Eds.), *Measuring Justice: Primary Goods and Capabilities.* Cambridge: Cambridge University Press.
[http://dx.doi.org/10.1017/CBO9780511810916.011]

Smith, A. (1759). *The Theory of Moral Sentiments.* Retrieved from: https://archive.org/details/theoryofmoralsentiments_0910_librivox
[http://dx.doi.org/10.1093/oseo/instance.00042831]

Smith, A. (1763). *Lectures on Justice, Police, Revenue and Arms.* Retrieved from: http://oll.libertyfund.org/titles/smith-lectures-on-justice-police-revenue-and-arms-1763

Smith, A. (1776). *An Inquiry into the Nature and Causes of the Wealth of Nations*. Retrieved from: http://www.ifaarchive.com/pdf/smith_-_an_inquiry_into_the_nature_and_causes_of_the_wealth_of_nations%5B1%5D.pdf
[http://dx.doi.org/10.1093/oseo/instance.00043218]

Smith, A. (1812). *The Works of Adam Smith. With an Account of his Life and Writings*. Retrieved from: https://archive.org/details/worksadamsmithw00stewgoog

Smith, A. (1976-1983). *The Glasgow Edition of the Works and Correspondence of Adam Smith*. Retrieved from: http://oll.libertyfund.org/groups/58

Tobin, J. (1958). Liquidity Preference as Behaviour Towards Risk. *Rev. Econ. Stud, 25*(1), 65-66.
[http://dx.doi.org/10.2307/2296205]

Tobin, J. (1961). Money, Capital, and Other Stores of Value. *Am. Econ. Rev, 51*(2), 26-37.

Tobin, J. (1963). Commercial Banks as Creators of 'Money. In: Carson, D., (Ed.), *Banking and Monetary Studies* (pp. 408-419). Homewood, IL: Richard D. Irwin.

Tobin, J. (1969). *A General Equilibrium Approach to Monetary Theory.*
[http://dx.doi.org/10.2307/1991374]

Tobin, J. (1975). Keynesian Models of Recession and Depression. *American Economic Review: AEA Papers and Proceedings, 65*(2), 175-182.

Tobin, J. Essays in Economics, 4 volumes. Cambridge, MA: MIT Press.

Tobin, J. (1982). The Commercial Banking Firm: A Simple Model. *Scand. J. Econ, 84*(4), 495-530.
[http://dx.doi.org/10.2307/3439515]

Tobin, J. (1984). On the Efficiency of the Financial System. *Lloyds Bank Review, 153*, 1-15.

Tobin, J. (1987). *Policies for Prosperity: Essays in a Keynesian Mode.* Cambridge, MA: MIT Press.

AUTHOR INDEX

SUBJECT INDEX

www.ingramcontent.com/pod-product-compliance
Lightning Source LLC
LaVergne TN
LVHW070936210926
848482LV00003B/250